CULTURE

CHRIS JENKS

London and New York

First published 1993
by Routledge
11 New Fetter Lane, London EC4P 4EE

Simultaneously published in the USA and Canada
by Routledge
29 West 35th Street, New York, NY 10001

Reprinted 1994, 1995

© 1993 Chris Jenks

Typeset in Times by Intype, London
Printed and bound in Great Britain by
Clays Ltd., St Ives PLC

British Library Cataloguing in Publication Data
A catalogue record for this book is available from
the British Library

Library of Congress Cataloguing in Publication Data
A catalogue record for this book is available from the Library of Congress

ISBN 0-415-07278-6

Contents

The author

Chris Jenks has taught undergraduates on courses in communication studies and sociology for a decade, helped to establish and teach a successful masters degree programme in Communication, Culture and Society and taught courses on cultural reproduction. He is currently Senior Lecturer in Sociology at Goldsmiths' College, University of London. His major publications include *Worlds Apart – Readings for a Sociology of Education* (with Beck, Keddie and Young), *Rationality, Education and the Social Organization of Knowledge, The Sociology of Childhood, Cultural Reproduction* and *Durkheim, Art and Representation* (with Smith – forthcoming).

Acknowledgements

I would like to thank my friends Malcolm Barnard, Stephen Featherstone, Paul Filmer, Dick Hebdige, Mike Phillipson, John Smith and Dave Walsh, for the ideas they have generated and misconceptions dispelled throughout the years, all of which have contributed to the present state of my thinking. More specifically I offer thanks to Justin Lorentzen and Don Slater for their particular suggestions, advice and recommendations on this book.

Finally, and of special note, I extend my gratitude to Ian Heywood for 'friendship, theorizing and climbing' but also for his scrupulous attention to a previous draft of this manuscript and his continued support.

I would like to hold them collectively responsible for any failures in argument, weaknesses in conceptualization or substantive omissions from this work; however, convention demands that I now exonerate them from all such blame and shoulder it myself.

Introduction

Raymond Williams informs us that 'Culture is one of the two or three most complicated words in the English language'[1] and while he is never quite good enough to tell us what the other one, or perhaps two, might be I have no principled, let alone experientially based, reasons to demur on this point. The idea of culture embraces a range of topics, processes, differences and even paradoxes such that only a confident and wise person would begin to pontificate about it and perhaps only a fool would attempt to write a book about it – thus I begin. The concept is at least complex and at most so divergent in its various applications as to defy the possibility, or indeed the necessity, of any singular designation. It is nevertheless real in its significations both in everyday language and in its increasingly broad currency within the fashionable discourses of the modern academy.

This last point concerning the contemporary (re)emergence of interest in the conceptualization of culture, particularly within intellectual circles, is perhaps a good one from which to proceed. Every generation, it is rightly supposed, creates new objects, ideas and meanings – such is the nature of social change, for better or worse. However, preceding generations and later the reflexive investigations of historical studies, quite often assert that far from such creations embodying originality they are rather re-invocations of ideas or states of affairs that went before. This is not some crude espousal of a doctrine of eternal returns nor even an argument in support of a theory of the universal properties of social life. What I am recommending is that any such creativity must be understood in relation to its social context. Just so with 'culture'. It has not been invented in the latter part of the twenti-eth century; however, the contemporary upsurge in interest in the idea of culture must surely tell us something about the times we are living through. Part of my purpose in this account of the concept of culture will be to place it within a history of ideas; part also will be to review and synthesize different arguments and perspectives on the topic, and to look critically at the charac-ter and status of some of the modern debates around the issue.

These caveats are meant, in part, as a warning to the reader that within this text it is not my intention to examine just the vanguard of heady exotica in contemporary 'cultural studies'. I am a sociologist and I approach culture as primarily a sociological problem. I also believe that the concept of culture has a history and that it does so in relation to traditions of thought; all of which are, in turn, located in social structures. An investigation of such traditions and their social contexts will take us both far and wide: into the realms of European philosophy, with Kant and Hegel writ large, through the classical theories of sociology and cul-tural anthropology stemming from the beginning of the century, and up to modern hermeneutics and structuralisms. We will also, of necessity, take in the contributions of Romanticism and literary criticism along with critical aesthetics – all of which have added to the present state of our understanding of and ways of relating to 'culture'. It is my conscious intention to ground the idea of culture in established theory and thus, I anticipate, to demon-strate the origins, the problematics, the desire and the energy that motivates whatever is most contemporary in the ever growing body of books and journals dedicated to the topic. This is no sleight nor denigration of the 'new'. The vigorous emergence of cultural theory over the last decade is both an exciting develop-ment within the social sciences, and an interesting topic for those very disciplines. The traditions of thought that I am seeking to honour and reveal are 'living' traditions; they are not presented here as curios or exhibits in a museum.

My projected strategy is not based on a stance of ritualistic obeisance to my tradition but on a serious re-reading of that tradition animated by both criticism and respect. In this way I shall reveal some unexpected resemblances, homologies and resonances between schools of thought usually regarded as radically different if not openly hostile to one another. The newcomer to the field, or indeed the informed reader, will be quite capable of engaging with the most recently published debates and controversies over culture, at some level. My purpose here is to present such readers with a map of our existing territory, and a guide to that map in the form of a classification, or a morphology, of the central concepts and ideas in terms of their meanings, origins and overlaps. Once equipped with such a guide the interested stranger can become familiar, a 'local resident', and thereby embark on a better informed and more critical appreciation of tomorrow's news in the study of culture.

If this work succeeds it should contrive to render its own classification of ideas already outmoded or inappropriate for the emergent theorist. It will also, I trust, have shown this classification as itself a cultural practice involving critical reading, judgement and discernment, and adherence to an intellectual discipline (a symbolic culture).

In a television interview towards the end of 1991 the playwright David Hare referred to 'the idea that is now very popular . . . that Bob Dylan is just as good a poet as Keats'. He went on not to agree with such thinking but to cite it as an instance of a modern populist ideology concerning the equivalence of all cultural products. Hare's position was quite the contrary, indeed he appeared to be rallying the latent elitism within our society that has been silenced by the current overbearing political correctness of a public opinion which, masquerading as democracy, is in fact only the fear, or at worst the inability, to make critical judgements concerning matters of taste and quality. Hare's view was that culture concerned absolute standards, standards which demand the greatest effort and engagement on the part of its creator and its audience. Culture, from this perspective, does not merely entertain, it enriches and uplifts; it embodies a struggle in its inception and in its apprehension which itself involves the maximization or even the extension of human potential. As such, culture is not to be treated lightly; it cannot be released into a pool of generalities or dissolved within a postmodern mood of relativism.

Now, I begin with this instance because of what it points us towards when we address the concept of culture. Interesting as Hare's views may be, the arguments have been largely prefigured in debates conducted by such eminent figures as Wordsworth and Coleridge, T. S. Eliot and Leavis, and more recently Raymond Williams and Richard Hoggart; some of which we shall examine later. However, when Hare made his point public the effect was to reopen a series of strategies for differentiation that exist both within the intellectual field and also the collective consciousness. As John Naughton, critic for the *Observer* put it:

> Much to Mr. Hare's surprise this entirely unremarkable judgement caused quite a stir. Men with moustaches and pork-pie hats came up to him in the street and exhorted him to keep up the good work. He became the folk hero among taxi drivers and others who think that the country is going to the dogs. It was, they thought, high time that someone made a stand against the prevailing tide of cultural relativism and its doctrine that whatever turns you on is OK.
>
> The relativists, for their part, regarded Mr. Hare with angry distaste, and muttered into their muesli. The acrid truth he had uttered left an unpleasant stench in their progressive nostrils. It opened up the terrifying prospect of a return to a state in which rigorous value judgements might become the norm, in which people might say that some works of art were better than others rather than being simply more or less 'interesting'.[2]

What we can hear in this quote, distilled through hyperbole, is a whole series of attitudes, or rather, discourses, about identity and difference within society. We can hear social class, nationalism, political allegiance and generation; all in relation to lifestyles and finally all in relation to an implicit theory of cultural value.

Should we say that the argument here revolves around the opposition between absolutism and relativism? This is certainly an important dichotomy in the history and understanding of culture, and one that occurs in the vocabulary of the contributors to this exchange. Or should we say that this binary is only a mask for the true difference at work, which is between elitism and egalitarianism? Though this may be nothing more than an attempt to politicize a debate about standards. Conversely, to ignore such a point could be seen as an attempt to depoliticize an otherwise purely ideological contradiction. This political dimension would also seem to be an important level of consideration in the understanding of culture. But what if we move to a more analytical level and suggest that the real difference at work is one between evaluation and description, and culture is a concept that fulfils either one of these tasks? Such a position has been maintained in the justification of the differentiation between the two dominant academic uses of the concept 'culture'. What I shall say at this point is that each of these considerations, and others to follow, contributes to our problematic: 'what do we mean by culture?' and 'how is the term used?'

'Man does not have a nature, but a history . . .' (Ortega y Gasset).

NOTES

[1] R. Williams, *Keywords*, London: Fontana (1976).
[2] *Observer*, 1 December 1991.

1

Origins of the concept of 'culture' in philosophy and the literary tradition

> . . . there is no such thing as a human nature independent
> of culture. Men without culture would not be the clever
> savages of Golding's *Lord of the Flies* thrown back upon
> the cruel wisdom of their animal instincts; nor would
> they be the nature's noblemen of Enlightenment primitiv-
> ism or even, as classical anthropological theory would
> imply, intrinsically talented apes who had somehow failed
> to find themselves. They would be unworkable mon-
> strosities with very few useful instincts, fewer recognis-
> able sentiments, and no intellect: mental basket cases.[1]

So what then is this thing called culture? What is this mediation
that appears to rob 'man' of his nature and locate his action and
practices within an endowment of socially produced symbolic
forms? Culture itself, whatever its facticity, is also a concept with
a history, some of which we shall try to trace in the chapters that
follow. It is hoped that we will not succumb to any one 'origin
myth' for, as anthropologists would tell us in relation to primitive
cosmologies, such devices only serve to exercise closure, they
silence debate and controversy and, usually, justify the existing

rationale for the status quo; nevertheless we will 'dig around' for sources, albeit competing ones.

One compelling account, and one that I shall trade off because it is symbiotic with the upsurge of social theory, is that the idea of 'culture' can be witnessed emerging in the late eighteenth century and on into the nineteenth century as part of, and largely as a reaction to, the massive changes that were occurring in the structure and quality of social life. These changes, at the social, political and personal levels, were both confusing and disorientating; and at least controversial. Such changes, through industrialization and technology, were unprecedented in human experience; they were wildly expansionist, horizons were simply consumed; grossly productive, for good and ill; and both understood and legitimated through an ideology of progress. The social structure was politically volatile, being increasingly and visibly divisive. This was a situation brought about through the new forms of ranking and hierarchy that accompanied the proliferating division of labour, being combined with the density and proximity of populations, through urbanization, and the improved system of communications. In one sense the overall aesthetic quality of life, compared with the previously supposed rural idyll, was threatened by the machine-like excesses of industrial society. There was an increasing gap between the creative and the productive, formulated for materialism by Marx as 'alienation', and for the Romantic-idealist tradition by Carlyle as a loss of the folk purity of a past era. The machine was viewed as devouring the natural character of humankind, a call to be later echoed in the work of the Frankfurt School, Benjamin's 'Age of Mechanical Reproduction', even Marcuse's sense of 'one-dimensionality', and finally the cri de coeur of Baudrillard's evocation of postmodernism with its horror of simulacra. Whereas we began with 'culture' mediating between 'man' and Nature, it can now be seen to mediate between 'man' and Machine. This provides us with several available 'meanings' of culture.

Another account looks back to classical society. 'Civilization', deriving from the latin *civis*, is a term descriptive of a state of belonging to a collectivity that embodied certain qualities, albeit self-appointed, which distinguished it from the 'mass' or more lowly state of being typified as that of the 'barbarian'. Such was the Ancient Greek and Roman sense of identification with Nation and State.

In this context the idea of 'culture' is not so much descriptive as metaphoric and derives, philologically, from the agricultural or horticultural processes of cultivating the soil and bringing fauna and flora into being through growth. The former concept, 'civilization', is descriptive of a kind of stasis, a membership, a belonging, indeed a status once achieved not to be relinquished; the latter, 'culture', is resonant with other ideas of emergence and change, perhaps even transformation. Thus we move to ideas of socialization as 'cultivating' the person, education as 'cultivating' the mind and colonization as 'cultivating' the natives. All of these uses of culture, as process, imply not just a transition but also a goal in the form of 'culture' itself; it is here that hierarchical notions begin to emerge such as the 'cultured person' or 'cultivated groups or individuals' and even the idea of a 'high culture', all of which reduce the metaphoricity of process and begin to coalesce with the original notion of a descriptive state of being not essentially unlike the formative idea of civilization itself. However, we are provided with another set of 'meanings' for culture.

Sociologists and anthropologists have come to account for the concept of culture in a variety of ways. In its most general and pervasive sense it directs us to a consideration of all that which is symbolic: the learned, ideational aspects of human society. In an early sense culture was precisely the collective noun used to define that realm of human being which marked its ontology off from the sphere of the merely natural. To speak of the cultural was to reaffirm a philosophical commitment to the difference and particularity that is 'humankind'. Animals, even the chattering dolphins, 'do' nature, while human beings inevitably transform their world into, and by way of, a series of symbolic representations. The symbolic then satisfies and absorbs the projections of human beings into objects and states of affairs that are different, and it also acts as a mediator between these two provinces. We no longer confront the natural, as if we were continuous with it, as it is supposed that animals do. We now meet with the natural and, indeed, experience it as preformed, through our vocabulary of symbols which are primarily linguistic but increasingly elaborate out into other forms like custom, convention, habit and even artefact. The symbolic representations that constitute human knowing are, in their various groupings, classifications and manifestations, the *cultural*. The very idea of culture therefore generates a concept which, at one level, provides a principle of unification for the peoples of the world;

including those who once have and also those who continue to populate the world through time and across space. Culture then, for early anthropology, was the common domain of the human; it distinguished our behaviour from that of other creatures and it provided a conceptual break with the dominant explanatory resource of biological and, latterly, genetic determinism. From this happy state of egalitarian one-ness through the aegis of culture – the very inspiration for cultural anthropology – the story takes a different turn and we move into accounts of diffusion, stratification, hierarchy and relativism, still clinging to the unrevised central concept of culture. Some of these tributaries and their ramifications we shall explore later in the text.

The dominant European linguistic convention equates 'culture' largely with the idea of 'civilization': they are regarded as synonymous. Both ideas may be used interchangeably with integrity in opposition to notions of that which is vulgar, backward, ignorant or retrogressive. Within the German intellectual tradition, to which we shall be repeatedly drawn, a different and particular sense of culture emerged that was to assume a dominant place in our everyday understandings. This was the Romantic, elitist, view that culture specified the pinnacle of human achievement. Culture, in this sense, came to specify that which is remarkable in human creative achievement. Rather than encapsulating all human symbolic representation German *Kultur* pointed us exclusively to levels of excellence in fine art, literature, music and individual personal perfection. The main body, or in this formulation, the residue of what we have previously meant as culture, was to be understood in terms of the concept of *Zivilisation*. This distinction, by no means fine, in many ways reflected the dichotomy provided by Kantian philosophy between the realms of 'value' and 'fact', and was generative of two different ways of understanding and relating to the world. These realms were systematically promoted into an antagonism at one level utterly esoteric and of the peculiar interests of philosophers only, but at another level the very grounds of the spurious doctrine of racial superiority that provided an impetus to the Holocaust. We will discuss this divide later in relation to idealism and materialism and cultural stratification, but we might note here that such distinctions also gave rise to the belief that the human spirit (perhaps the *Geist* itself) came under successive threat with the advent and advance of modernity and the inexorable process of material development which, it was supposed, gave rise to an increasingly anonymous and amorphous urban mass society; thus linking with our initial argument. The impersonal, yet evil, forces of standardization, industrialization and technologies of mass production became the analytic target for the Romantic neo-Marxist criticism of the Frankfurt School within their theories of aesthetics, mass communication and mass society, and also in the early sociology of culture propounded by Norbet Elias with his ideas of the 'civilizing process'.

Within the confines of British and American social theory the concept of culture has been understood in a far more pluralist sense and applied, until relatively recently, on a far more sparing basis. Although culture is a familiar term within our tradition and can be employed to summon up holistic appraisals of the ways of life of a people, their beliefs, rituals and customs, it is not most common. We social scientists are rather more accustomed to mobilizing such batteries of understanding into 'action sets'. That is, we tend to use more specific concepts like, for example, 'value systems' (even 'central value systems'), 'patterns of belief', 'value orientations' or more critical notions like 'ideologies'. Culture, to British and American social theorists, tends to have been most usefully applied as a concept of differentiation within a collectivity rather than a way of gathering. That is to say that the concept has become artfully employed in, for example, the sociology of knowledge that Mannheim recommends, and also in the spectrum of perspectives on the sociology of deviance – ranging from Parsonian theory through to symbolic interactionism – in the manner of 'subculture'. A subculture is the way of defining and honouring the particular specification and demarcation of special or different interests of a group of people within a larger collectivity. So just as classical sociology in the form of Tönnies or Durkheim, or indeed Comte, had recognized that the composition of the overall collective life emerged through the advance of the division of labour – by dint of the fragile integration through interdependence of a whole series of smaller, internally cohesive, social units – so also does modern social theory by articulating the specific mores of these minor groups, albeit often as 'non-normative' or even 'deviant'. This dispersion of subcultures is at the base of what we might mean by a 'pluralist' view of culture; it is modern and democratic and shies away from all of the excesses of a grand systems theory with all of its incumbent conservative tendencies and its implicit 'oversocialized conception of man'.[2] Such thinking succumbs, however, to the problem of order. Without a coherent, overall theory of culture (which still, in many senses, eludes us), it is hard to conceive of how consensus is maintained within a modern society. In response to precisely this problem, contemporary Marxism has generated the 'dominant ideology thesis' which supposes that varieties of hegemonic strategies of mass media and political propaganda create a distorted illusion of shared concerns in the face of the real and contentious divisions that exist between classes, genders, ethnic groups, geographical regions and age groups. Such a thesis is by no means universally accepted within the social sciences and in many ways the more recent explosion of interest in and dedication to the schizophrenic prognosis of postmodernisms positively accelerates the centrifugal tendencies of the cultural particles.

I will attempt to summarize some of the above accounts of the genesis of our concept 'culture' through a four-fold typology.

1 Culture as a cerebral, or certainly a cognitive category: culture becomes intelligible as a general state of mind. It carries with it the idea of perfection, a goal or an aspiration of individual human achievement or emancipation. At one level this might be a reflection of a highly individualist philosophy and at another level an instance of a philosophical commitment to the particularity and difference, even the 'chosenness' or superiority of humankind. This links into themes of redemption in later writings, from Marx's false consciousness to the melancholy science of the Frankfurt School. In origin we will see it mostly in the work of the Romantic literary and cultural criticism of Coleridge and Carlyle and latterly Matthew Arnold.

2 Culture as a more embodied and collective category: culture invokes a state of intellectual and/or moral development in society. This is a position linking culture with the idea of civilization and one that is informed by the evolutionary theories of Charles Darwin (1809–82) and informative of that group of social theorists now known as the 'early evolutionists' who pioneered anthropology, with their competitive views on 'degeneration' and 'progress', and linked the endeavour to nineteenth-century imperialism. This notion nevertheless takes the idea of culture into the province of the collective life, rather than the individual consciousness.

3 Culture as a descriptive and concrete category; culture viewed as the collective body of arts and intellectual work within any

one society: this is very much an everyday language usage of the term 'culture' and carries along with it senses of particularity, exclusivity, elitism, specialist knowledge and training or socialization. It includes a firmly established notion of culture as the realm of the produced and sedimented symbolic; albeit the esoteric symbolism of a society.

4 Culture as a social category; culture regarded as the whole way of life of a people: this is the pluralist and potentially democratic sense of the concept that has come to be the zone of concern within sociology and anthropology and latterly, within a more localized sense, cultural studies.

A PHILOSOPHICAL TRADITION: ARISTOTLE, LOCKE, VICO, TURGOT AND BENTHAM

Although, as one major strand in our modern thinking displays, culture is often understood in relation to achievements within the realms of art and literature, the nearest classical approximation to our present-day view is found not in the study of aesthetics but in moral philosophy. Aristotle's *Nicomachean Ethics* reveals an understanding of human excellence, shared normative expectations as evaluative criteria, and a sense of the natural disposition of humankind to such achievement. The work rests on an essential teleology that all things are to be understood in terms of their purposes but their purposes are not wilful, or merely contingent, they are inherent in the nature of things. The 'good' for Aristotle is that which all things aim at and the 'good' for humankind is happiness in the form of virtuous action. This is the true realization of human nature and all other conduct falls short of our true potential. The virtue or excellence of a human being is achieved through the maximization of the potentialities of our nature and as people are essentially rational creatures their 'good' is found in the activity of the soul in accordance with reason. Although Aristotle is offering a type of naturalism it is in no sense a reductionist argument because it enables the important difference between empirical reality and a sense of the ideal – this is a conceptual gap that is often relevant to the analyses and recommendations of cultural theorists.

In our search for origins an unlikely source but, I believe, a genuine one, is to be found in John Locke's *An Essay Concerning Human Understanding* (1690). Although he never invokes a concept of culture he does forcefully indicate the predisposition of human consciousness to the assimilation of the baggage of collective knowledge. Of course, Locke's treatise is more familiarly known as a landmark in the history of British philosophy. It provides us with the 'tabula rasa', the empty bucket theory of mind, which once united with Berkeley's radical subjectivism and Hume's sceptical inductionism sends us on the arid path to modern empiricism with its compulsive and dogmatic adhesion to the centrality of the senses. However, the critique of the a priori in the first book of Locke's essay tells a second story. When he shows us that children and halfwits do not appear to conform to the rules of thinking and behaving that are supposedly 'stamped upon the mind of men' he is clearing the space for a knowledge that is pluralistic and diffused, but more locally, shared, learned and transmitted.

The thought of the eighteenth-century philosopher Giovanni Battista Vico was directly in line with the demands of the Enlightenment project. His *New Science* (1744) addressed itself wholeheartedly to the range of phenomena gathered by Pope's dictum that 'the proper study of mankind is man'. However, whereas the epistemological awakenings of the Enlightenment encouraged the study of human affairs through the objectivities and mechanicisms of the 'hard' sciences, Vico's new science was clearly the precursor of social theory; it opted to investigate human 'being' in terms of its own symbolic creations. This investigation, or 'philology' as Vico referred to it, would look to what humankind had sedimented through its history, its mode of communication, its belief systems and its legal conventions. In short, many of Vico's topics for empirical study we would today include as elements in our definition of culture. Although operating with a rationalist scepticism in the manner of Descartes, who having employed the *cogito* to prove the existence of Self then pressed on to prove the existence of God and finally targeted Nature, Vico's goals were far less ambitious. He left the production and comprehension of Nature to God and restricted the New Science to knowing the knowable, namely, that which Man himself had created; what we have come to call culture.

> . . . the world of civil society has certainly been made by men and its principles are therefore to be found within the modification of our own human mind.

> Because of the indefinite nature of the human mind,

wherever it is lost in ignorance, man makes himself the measure of all things.

When men are ignorant of the natural causes producing things, they attribute their own nature to them.[3]

It is not surprising given the content of these brief passages that certain forms of contemporary structuralism have also traced their roots back to Vico. However, our primary interest in such utterances is that Vico is speaking of the symbolic transformation of the 'natural' into the 'cultural'. The history of human culture and civilization attests to the triumph of the inherent tendencies of the human constitution. Man has ceased to crawl and act like a wild beast because of the creative encoding of his species being. The New Science begins with a series of philosophical assertions on the basis of which human purpose, progress and cultural evolution are ensured. They are redolent with a dynamism and a creative potential that humankind, it is argued, projects into that which is other than itself and therefore orders and tames it; the idea resonates with Lévi-Strauss's view on the practice and function of primitive cosmologies. The resonance amplifies when Vico next turns to an analysis of mythology in order to account for human prehistory (itself a myth that prefigures all social theory in a variety of forms, from Durkheim's primitive horde, through Rousseau's primitive but gentle savage, to Marx's primitive communism). The outcome of this analysis is a theory of social en-culturation, that is, all societies must pass through three stages: the age of Gods, the age of Heroes and the age of Men (a gradient not essentially distant from Comte's epistemological evolution from theology, through metaphysics to positivism). Corresponding to these three stages are three kinds of customs: belief systems, laws and commonwealths. The human persona transforms, in parallel, from ferocity, through pride into reason. This is surely an early parable concerning culture as the essence of human goodness.

The first clearly recognizable formulation of our concept 'culture', albeit unnamed, is provided through the excavations into European philosophy of the anthropologist Marvin Harris. He reveals a succinct passage from the work of Anne Robert Jacques Turgot dated 1750 which states:

Possessor of a treasure of signs which he has the faculty of multiplying into infinity, he [man] is able to assure the retention of his acquired ideas, to communicate them to other men, and to transmit them to his successors as a constantly expanding heritage.[4]

This may prove to be a definition that it is hard to improve upon.

Bentham's writing in *An Introduction to the Principles of Morals and Legislation* (1789) can be read as a treatise in amelioration, that is a well-meaning ethical foundation for the adjustment of the individual will to the onslaught and ravages of its times. As the exponentially reproductive processes and structures of industrialization began to produce *for* the population, so also did they produce at the expense *of* the population. The increasing availability of commodities on the market place of free enterprise was an idea easily offset by the concentrations of human misery that were being routinely invested in their manufacture. Adam Smith's economic principle of 'the division of labour' and its social reality in the reorganization and orientation of human relationships was leading many diverse thinkers to contemplate the erosion of both personal creativity and the human spirit, and also the necessity for a ruling system of cohesion and concerted change. This was clearly giving birth to doctrines of revolution, revision, Romanticism and conservation. Bentham's 'principle of utility' which has become diluted into a modern version of keeping everybody happy, is in fact to be heard in relation to a necessary backdrop of pain. He states:

> Nature has placed mankind under the governance of two sovereign masters, pain and pleasure. . . . The principle of utility recognises this subjection, and assumes it for the foundation of that system, the object of which is to rear the fabric of felicity by the hands of reason and the law.[5]

Thus, given the essential conditions of being, which are as they are, people must adjust to life, gain contentment from it and get on with it. This is a culture of functional utility. So Bentham dedicates the body of his writing to an understanding of human psychology in as much as it brings illumination to our theories of social control. A major part of his work and interests reveals him as a penologist, seeking to generate the rational bases for an efficient correctional machine in the form of the modern society (symbolized through his 'dream prison', the panopticon).

THE LITERARY-ROMANTIC TRADITION: COLERIDGE, CARLYLE AND ARNOLD

In dramatic contrast to Bentham and writing perhaps a quarter of a century after him we find Coleridge (1772–1834), not this time in the guise of poet but rather as literary and social critic. He appears to be generating an oppositional theory of the necessity of human self-expression in the face of modernity and thus making a significant contribution to our current understanding of the concept of culture, perhaps inspired by but not prefigured in the mechanics of utilitarianism. Coleridge in his *Constitution of Church and State* (1837) espouses a Romantic vision of the capability of and necessity for humankind to pursue the goal of spiritual perfection. This goal is what he will refer to as 'cultivation', 'the harmonious development of those qualities and faculties that characterize our humanity'.[6] It is in this context that we find the first articulate application of the verb 'to cultivate', which until the eighteenth century had been used exclusively in relation to gardening or agriculture, to the organization and development of human worth, self-expression and authenticity. Through Coleridge we attend to the generation and nurture of the symbolic attributes of people that mark them off ontologically and imbue them with a transcendent purpose. Humankind, in this mould, is no longer subject to the vagaries of the natural environment but is rather in touch with an ideal similarly celebrated through the doctrine of Christianity, an ideal of the perfection of the spirit. Cultivation now directs us to a condition of the mind, and culture thus enters the language as an essential disposition of persons. However, to consider this departure within the vocabulary of the social sciences, we are not being offered a metaphysical version of methodological individualism. Coleridge is not pointing to the unique and isolated self as the source of this motivation to achieve perfection, but rather to a condition of the collective. We may have moved from the compulsive external constraints of the utilitarian world to a state of inner being, but an inner being in the context of and as an instance of the social world. Coleridge is surely writing about the social conditions that will enable the realization of human perfection, within a set of rapidly transforming historical conditions that seem dedicated to instability or are, at least, contradictory to all aspiration towards any positive entelechy. These social conditions are the institutions that provide continuity in a changing world, institutions like the church and the state in the title of his essay.

Coleridge suggests that institutions both provide for the possibility of human endeavour and offer support to the initiative and struggles of particular individuals. This unification of individual purpose and collective manifestation would make for a yardstick against which the 'good' of human cultivation might measure, and thus resist, the consuming mechanicism of the new industrial order. Two realms thus emerge from this period, the inner, 'natural' state of human cultivation, gravitated towards perfection, and the external, material and mechanical metamorphoses that are directed by the inevitable forces of modernity that we call 'progress'. These realms are coterminous but utterly antagonistic. This somewhat Kantian 'counteraction' of forces, as it is referred to by Coleridge, the tension between the inside and the outside, the poet counselling nature even as he is directed by it, is a process generated by the active imagination. He regards the imagination as that 'essentially vital' driving force which 'dissolves, diffuses, dissipates' the very world that threatens to engulf it.

Coleridge was a leading British exponent of this theory of aesthetics that stemmed from the philosophical writings of Immanuel Kant. Such thinking transformed the previously entrenched dualism between the creative artist and nature, prevalent in the eighteenth century, into a complex, circular contingency of infinite counteraction. One might almost suggest an appearance of a theory of dialectics in the act of creation, but certainly an original view of a culture involving the simultaneous deposition and apprehension of symbolic representations. Such representations, be they essays, poems or other artefacts, thus acquired a troublesome epistemological status, which Coleridge referred to as a 'tertium aliquid'. This is an entity which is neither subject nor object but rather 'an interpenetration of the counteracting powers, partaking of both'. Such elements of what we might call culture are to be regarded as neither idea nor tangible entity; they have a special quality that resides between these two realms.

Culture, or rather cultivation, was for Coleridge and all subsequent thinking on the topic, a process, intangible but real in its consequences, a goal, an ideal and most of all a condition of the mind in social life. It must be safeguarded, preserved, aspired towards and worked for. Such a dwelling place for the human condition cannot be taken for granted. The mundane inevitability of everyday life is not culture, it is the history of civilization which may be held to account alongside the achievements of cultivation. These two will never be confused again. Culture becomes the counterforce in the face of the destructive tendencies of industrialization and mass society. Civilization becomes the ally of these destructive forces. It is in this way that we can reconcile the demolition of beautiful buildings to make way for supermarkets and high rise offices with the march of civilization, while we preserve our cultural standards in the tradition of western architecture.

Coleridge further suggests the formation of an elite group within society who shall be charged with the responsibility of upholding and pursuing the necessary ideal of culture. This he refers to as the 'clerisy', a secular church. Such notions are alive, yet vestigial, in the modern intelligentsia who, in part, preserve the goodness of the past and project it as a measure of the present through the concepts of tradition and discipline.

Culture is now liberated. It may, from this release by Coleridge and with the complicity of Ruskin, come to be identified with the arts. It may, from this same emancipatory source, come to be derided by certain modern thinkers as the ideology of the intellectual classes. Whatever, it will no longer be conflated with civilization; it is a parallel but different process.

The discourse of culture is a relatively new phenomenon in the history of ideas.

Thomas Carlyle (1795–1881) the Scottish historian, philosopher and critic published his influential essay *Signs of the Times* in 1829 in which he succinctly laid out his views of the state of modernity. Influenced and accelerated by Coleridge's thought he shared and amplified many of Coleridge's ideas in the form of social criticism and to this end combined, along with Arnold, to generate a solid foundation from which to appreciate, appraise and uphold the notion of culture. Engulfed as he was, in common with all intellectuals of the time, by the sheer material presence of industrialism and its effects on the environment and, more significantly, on the lifestyle, creative propensity and patterning of relationships of the populace, he defined his era disparagingly as 'not an Heroical, Devotional, Philosophical, or Moral Age, but, above all others, the Mechanical Age'.[7] The relations of craft and labour were being overcome by the politics and economics of speed and technology. Human labour was becoming routinized and 'fitted' to its particular function in the productive process as machines increasingly assumed the creative centre ground in society. A new spirit of political economy was abroad, one which revolved around the idea of 'capital' and its accumulation. Wealth was no longer a characteristic of a people but rather a force for dividing and polarizing the nation. Profit became the single, most formative motivating force for human conduct, even in the context of religious practice (a thesis that Max Weber would later expound in his work *The Protestant Ethic and the Spirit of Capitalism*). These thoughts prefigured Karl Marx's concept of 'alienation' and, in fact, elicited positive citation in Marx's own subsequent writing. Carlyle's critique was sweeping indeed. He refers this dominant process of mechanization not just to the organization and regimentation of the outside, the physical body, but also to the inside, the thoughts and feelings of the individual, a governing of the soul. It is as if he envisaged the modern person in a context of ergonomics and psychoanalysis! – a Romantic vision of loss, but nevertheless a prophetic one.

Just as Coleridge had constituted a combative dualism between the achievements that are human culture and the sedimentations that comprise the 'progress' of industrialism, Carlyle looked also to the 'two departments of man's activity'. These he designated as the 'dynamic' and the 'mechanical', which I shall later develop as the 'ideal' and the 'material'. The former, which concerns the inner life and the human spirit, is the necessary process of being, but one which, if left as a disembodied vision, leads to a languor of impracticality. The latter, the practice of doing in the world, accrues obvious material deposition. However, the contemporary preoccupation with this outer life leads to a decline of moral sentiment. When writing of the French Revolution as a clash between the 'old' and 'new' orders in European society, Carlyle states that 'It is towards a higher freedom than mere freedom from oppression by his fellow mortal, that man dimly aims' and this 'freedom' must surely be the liberation of a cultural 'dynamic' that runs through history.

Similarly, as Coleridge had proposed the necessity of an intellectual elite, which he termed the 'clerisy', to protect and propagate the excellence of a society, so also Carlyle recommends the leadership and heroism of a literary class to uphold the 'good' and to act as a force of change and renewal in the realm of culture. Carlyle is clear, and this is an important analytic moment in the conceptualization of 'culture', that the organization of modern society precludes the integration of 'culture' with the everyday activities of the population. A specialist, preservation group is required, though not sustained within modern society, because industrialization has forced the separation of the 'cultural' from the 'social'. The literary elite become not a class-based luxury but an historically forced necessity. Far from being moved in an hierarchical game, Carlyle is putting forward a forceful plea on behalf of democracy and pluralism. He is arguing that what stands as culture should be representative of the collective life of a people, but that this collective life should comprise more than the ugly relationships, mediated by money, that are enabled within the parameters provided by the modern industrial state. 'Is the condition of the English working people wrong?' he asks, and his answer is unambiguous.

In opposition to the oppressive post-Malthusian suggestions for alleviating the conditions of the working poor, like sexual abstinence, birth control and forced emigration, Carlyle put forward positive and integrative policies for mass, popular education. These policies would serve to reunite labour with thought, the outside with the inside, and reinstate the 'dynamic' of culture centrally within the 'mechanicism' of the social system.

The last of the great British nineteenth-century literary thinkers that I shall address, and perhaps the most important of them all in the context of the culture debate, is Matthew Arnold (1822–88). A contemporary of Carlyle, he too was much concerned with the 'processual' character of culture, for as well as being a poet and literary critic, he had a practical concern with the process of education; he was an inspector of schools.

Arnold, in common with his intellectual peers, was writing in response to, but also within, the ever-constraining parameters of an industrializing world. All of this group of writers were anxious to record and protest at what they saw as the corrosive effects of industrialism on the contemporary state of humanity but also, and most significantly, on the historically emergent force of human potential. The Victorians, in grand and Gothic style, had made a symbolic international announcement concerning the triumphant excellence of British achievement in the form of the Great Exhibition of 1851. This conspicuous celebration of self-appointed cultural superiority manifested itself through an array of artefacts ranging from architecture, design and textiles, through steam engines and factory machines to the level of aspidistras and bathroom china. This must have been an exercise in unconscious, projected bathos matched only by the broad spectrum of audience response and critical appraisal that it received. Henry Mayhew described it as 'the highest kind of school in which the highest knowledge is designed to be conveyed in the best possible manner, in combination with the highest amusement',[8] whereas John Ruskin considered the Exhibition to be made up of the ugly, the transitory and the banal. What was at stake here was not simply a range of local disagreements over what constitutes good taste but, as Arnold saw it, a serious competition concerning the dominant collective definition of what constitutes 'culture' itself. The outcome of this competition would have a significant impact on the future of western social life and thus Arnold committed himself to a resolution of this struggle and confusion over the realm of the cultural. The culmination of his thoughts and efforts in this endeavour he published as *Culture and Anarchy* (1869). Arnold was unequivocal in his views. Culture for him is 'high culture', it is the best that humankind can achieve, not an average or a descriptive category applicable to all human thought and production. It refers to the peak, which also provides the aspiration and similarly reveals the potential. Thus he tells us that 'Culture, which is the study of perfection, leads us . . . to conceive of true human perfection as a *harmonious* perfection, developing all sides of our humanity; and as a *general* perfection, developing all parts of our society.'[9] Prior to this powerful and optimistic assertion Arnold has informed us that his work is not only a manifesto, but also a remedy, given his diagnosis of the state of his world. Thus he recommends

> . . . culture as the great help out of our present difficulties; culture being the pursuit of our total perfection by means of getting to know, on all the matters which most concern us, the best which has been thought and said in the world; and, through this knowledge, turning a stream of fresh and free thought upon our stock notions and habits.[10]

It is not difficult here to sense the resonances between Arnold's thinking on culture and education and those of Plato concerning the socialization of his philosopher-kings:

> We would not have our Guardians grow up among representations of moral deformity, as in some foul pasture where, day by day, feeding on every poisonous weed

they would, little by little, gather insensibly a mass of
corruption in their very souls. Rather we must seek out
those craftsmen whose instinct guides them to whatsoever
is lovely and gracious; so that our young men, dwelling
in a wholesome climate, may drink in good from every
quarter, whence, like a breeze bearing health from happy
regions, some influence from noble works constantly falls
upon eye and ear from childhood upward, and imprecep-
tibly draws them into sympathy and harmony with
reason, whose impress they take . . . rhythm and harmony sink deep into the recesses of the soul and take
the strongest hold there, bringing that grace of body and
mind which is only to be found in one who is brought
up in the right way. Moreover, a proper training of this
kind makes a man quick to perceive any defects or ugli-
ness in art or in nature.[11]

The goal is perfection, the politic elitist, but the supposed ben-
eficiary the total collective life. The differences between Arnold
and his Hellenic predecessor are, as Arnold indicates, in the
historical context of their appeal to perfection. For Plato reason
was an emergent, 'inner state' of grace, for Arnold it had become
transformed into the post-Enlightenment forms of industrialization, it had become 'external' and 'mechanical'. The former
espouses a vanguard initiative, the latter a rearguard reaction.

Arnold's work can be heard as polemical and it certainly
bears a literary style that Williams[12] refers to as a 'soured romanticism'; he nevertheless produces a vivid and arresting analysis of
the profound and radical changes that were occurring in the forms
of knowledge, the kinds of technologies and the organization of
social relationships during that period. However, unlike J. S. Mill
and Carlyle whose work concerned and reflected upon culture,
to Arnold the primary issue of his age was culture itself. The sad
and threatening fact of modernity was, for Arnold, that this great
heritage and panacea, culture, was in tenuous and feeble hands.
The great body of the population, from rich to poor, seemed
incapable of registering and thus championing culture as the
central quality of being. In his exposition of the class system of
his time he finds no heroes and no redemption. The complacent
aristocracy, preoccupied with upholding the going system, he
designates 'Barbarians'; the abundant, self-seeking, entrepreneur-
ial middle classes he calls 'Philistines' for their over-investment

in the external characteristics of a mechanistic system; and the working classes, whom Marx would later elect to the status of salvationists, were for Arnold the 'populace', either aspiring towards the goals of the Philistines or rendered without potential through drudgery and degradation. The whole of the nation seemed without hope, prisoners of their epoch, mistakenly conflating the material and mechanical benefits of the modern age with the true purpose of being. We are told that 'Never did people believe anything more firmly than nine out of ten Englishmen at the present day believe that our greatness and welfare are proved by our being so very rich';[13] however, he acerbicly shatters this delusion when he continues that culture tells us to:

> [C]onsider these people, then, their way of life, their habits, their manners, the very tone of their voices; look at them attentively; observe the literature they read, the things which give them pleasure, the words which come forth out of their mouths, the thoughts which make the furniture of their minds; would any amount of wealth be worth having with the condition that one was to become just like these people by having it?[14]

The future, for Arnold, lies not in the habits and mentality of such a Zeitgeist, but rather in the form of a transcendent ideal of cultural perfection more clearly visible in the classical-Christian tradition and made manifest in the practices of the Renaissance. The purity that culture enables us to express and seek is not to have its infinity staled by mechanical custom and the routines of the division of labour. The vocationalist demands of utilitarianism are at once dispelled, education is not to be about the training of individuals for the functional requirements of their time and place, it is concerned with the process of growth into the best; and that process is 'culture'.

The choice is clear, between the central value of culture or the value-less disarray of anarchy. Having made the choice the way forward is through collective action. Arnold did not place the mission of culture in the hands of a special group of guardians like a 'clerisy' or a literary elite, nor did he see it as the private achievement of particular talented or privileged individuals; he saw that culture would be transmitted and become shared through the policies of the state, and his life work was concerned with establishing a new national system of general education.

NOTES

[1] C. Geertz, 'The impact of the concept of culture on the concept of man', in J. Platt (ed.), *New Views of the Nature of Man*, Chicago: University of Chicago Press (1965), pp. 112–13.

[2] D. Wrong, 'The oversocialized conception of man in modern sociology', *American Sociological Review* Vol. XXVI, April 1961.

[3] All three quotes from G. Vico, *The New Science* (1725/44).

[4] Quoted in M. Harris, *The Rise of Anthropological Theory*, New York: Thomas Y. Crowell (1968), p. 14.

[5] J. Bentham, *An Introduction to the Principles of Morals and Legislation* (1789).

[6] S. T. Coleridge, *The Constitution of Church and State* (1837).

[7] T. Carlyle, *Sign of the Times* (1829).

[8] H. Mayhew, *London Labour and the London Poor*, London (1856–61).

[9] M. Arnold, *Culture and Anarchy* (1869).

[10] Ibid.

[11] Plato, *The Republic*.

[12] R. Williams, *Culture and Society*, Harmondsworth: Penguin (1961).

[13] M. Arnold, op. cit.

[14] Ibid.

2

The relation between culture and social structure

The concept of a social structure is a continuous, yet often implicit, resource for sociological explanations. Indeed, we might go as far as to suggest that 'social structures' are that peculiar realm of phenomena, utterly intangible yet real, towards which sociology dedicates its practice. When Durkheim produced the manifesto for the discipline he marked out its territory, named and defined its facticity, and legislated for its most appropriate 'scientific' method. This facticity Durkheim called 'social facts', which are, themselves, no more than instances or icons of social structures at work. They make reference to orderly, patterned and enduring relationships that hold between elements of a society. These orderly formations exist in their own right, *sui generis*, so they are objective; they are external, thus not available for change at the will or caprice of particular individuals; and they are constraining or coercive in their impact on individual conduct. It is not possible to choose or think your way out of the pressures that social structures apply to social action. The supposed regularities, functional interrelations and equilibrium of such structures have led to the sustained application of 'organismic' analogies, as with Durkheim and the school of structural-functionalism; or to 'mechanistic' analogies, as with Parsons's cybernetic 'social system', being employed in sociological explanations.

Social structures, as theoretical devices, plant two problematics at the heart of sociology's project: (1) as they are both topic and resource for sociological accounts, the work must be teleological – it explains the social in terms of the social; and (2) as they are intangible, but employed causally, all explanations are made with reference to abstractions; it is for this reason that Durkheim himself had to resort to treating judicial codes and suicide rates as external indices of solidarity and integration.

What then of the relation between culture and social structure? My immediate response is to draw a clear distinction between the two and then to describe the various ways that theory has articulated the relation between them. However, nothing involving the concept of culture is so clear cut. Just as in many forms of discourse culture/civilization are used interchangeably, so in others culture/society/social structure are conflated, though not necessarily confused; indeed the idea of social structure as a theory of culture has created a major dividing line in the history of anthropological thought that we shall go on to consider. Let us begin by looking at three moments in the sociological tradition (all of which we shall revisit later) that would appear to differentiate culture from social structure. These moments are provided by Durkheim, Talcott Parsons and Marx, and all of them, in their different ways, see culture differentiated from social structure because it is viewed as an emergent process stemming from social action.

THE SYMBOLIC AND THE SEMIOTIC VIEWS OF CULTURE

Durkheim, having outgrown the blustering empiricism and polemical positivism of his early work, went on to develop a subtle, and almost dialectical, account of the development and maintenance of the social bond. In his later work, which is manifestly concerned with the explanation of primitive religious practice he is, in fact, arguing for the social genesis of epistemological categories – a truly sociological account of mind and knowledge. These are bold excursions into the realm of symbolism, the 'cultural', and demonstrations of its relation to the organization of human relationships, the 'social structural'. Durkheim argues that within simple societies, the precursors of complex modern societies, the differentiation between types of relationships is regulated by the intensity of affective experience. So just as we in complex societies 'feel closer' to our own immediate family than to our cousins, but perhaps 'closer' to them than to our neighbours, Durkheim informs us that this gradient of intensity is a primary experience of the primitive in relation to the established social groupings in his society, beginning with the oldest formations, the 'moieties', and passing through 'clans' to the most recent and most immediate relationships within the family and kinship group. Parallel with this 'affective' response is a pattern of 'cognitive' action in the form of religious practice. All religions, Durkheim tells us, divide the universe into the realms of the *sacred* and the *profane*; sacred symbols are condensed, pure, solidaristic and comforting whereas profane symbols are fragmenting and diffuse, dangerous and defiling and, above all, threatening to the sacred. The most primitive of religions also operates through *totemism* which involves the projection outwards of the group spirit onto an object or animal within the natural world; this natural object, or *totem*, then takes on sacred qualities, it becomes the source of identity and recognition of the particular group who selected it, it becomes their 'emblem' which they worship and revere. Just as the groups that go to make up a society stand in a fixed relation to one another so now, through their objectification in the form of totems, do the phenomena of the natural world. The compulsions of a coherent belief system thus give rise to a cosmology, and the social structure provides the model for the classificatory system.

'The first categories of things were categories of men.'[1] These 'primitive classifications', Durkheim continues, share all of the characteristics of scientific classificatory systems: they are used to provide order and coherence, they are branching, and they arrange phenomena hierarchically. More than this, we are assured, they have an absolute continuity with modern taxonomies where we still refer to phenomena as 'belonging to the same family'.

Durkheim had already established the autonomy and specificity of cultural symbols in his critiques of both idealist and empiricist epistemologies. Not all societies share the same classificatory systems, which would be the a priorist position, but within any one society the system is common which defies the individualism inherent in the empiricist theory of learning. There is a suggestion of a soft Kantian immanence here in the form of

Society itself but what Durkheim has opened up is the question of the relation between the social structure and the symbolic order. In order to transpose this relation into the context of an increasingly complex mode of differentiation in modern society Durkheim emphasizes the hermeneutic function of symbols rather than the referential function of signs. This distinction between the symbolic and the semiotic views of culture is important in avoiding essentialism and reductionism and is a point exercised by both Bernstein and Alexander[2] in more modern Durkheimian studies of culture.

Parsons, in his *Social System*,[3] provides a role for culture in legitimating social order and thus provides for its separate existence and yet integration with social structure. The social system is comprised of a social structure and three other subsystems, all of which are functionally interrelated and one of which is the 'cultural'. Whereas the economy drives the system and causes it to adapt to its environment, the family preserves and sustains the 'units' or the personalities within the system through socialization and care. The cultural system is charged with the prerequisites of *goal attainment* and *integration*. Essentially this means that culture has a central role in ensuring the equilibrium and internal homeostasis of the overall system. It has to provide a symbolic environment that is conducive to the social actors moving steadily towards their goals, and it has to maintain cooperation and integration between those same actors given the strains of goal attainment. The cultural, then, is supposed to be redolent with shared beliefs, interests and ideologies which serve to legitimate the social order. Within the realm of the cultural Parsons also sediments a principle of reciprocity, based on obligation, which ordains the relations between the individual and the collective, and thus provides a basis for the formulation of a common culture.

Unlike Durkheim's view of a culture comprised of constitutive and interpretive symbolism, the account of culture devised by Parsons relies on a singularity and fixity of meaning. Here the realms of *goal attainment* and *integration* are organized and directed in relation to a set of unequivocal signs, albeit at the level of abstraction. The members of the social system, the 'action units', have their conduct regulated through a collection of consensual aspirations, which he refers to as *central values*, and universal orientations, which he refers to as *pattern variables*. The conceptual matrix provided by these two accounts for all the possible needs and choices expressed by the individual. This singularity and fixity of meaning lead to what we mean by a 'semiotic' rather than a 'symbolic' view of culture. The 'signs' are referential rather than hermeneutic.

Finally Marx, for whom the social structure is organized in terms of the means and relations of production. Culture, within historical materialism, is clearly reducible to these economic factors, but emergent in the form of class consciousness. This dualistic causality is what we shall refer to as a dialectical conception of culture; the dialectic also ensures the differentiation of culture from social structure, even though there is, in Marxism, a firm sense of dependency, that is, in terms of cause and effect. The degree of dependency, which is exercised across the idealist-materialist spectrum of neo-Marxisms, reveals the possible liberation of Marxist accounts from the semiotic into the realm of the symbolic. The Marxist view of culture then, which tends to be preoccupied with realism and resistant to the symbolic excesses of modernism, sees it as the expression of a group consciousness. As such it is vociferous in relation to particular sets of interests and directed towards changing institutionalized social and political structures, although stasis is the normal condition of society, given that the dominant ideas of any particular historical period tend to be the ideas of the ruling groups. We will explore this set of ideas further in Chapter 4.

CULTURE AND STRUCTURE IN ANTHROPOLOGICAL THOUGHT

Now we turn to anthropology, a tradition rich in definitions of our concept culture; so we might do well to remember the warnings of Kroeber and Kluckholn: 'But a concept, even an important one, does not constitute a theory. . . . In anthropology at present we have plenty of definitions (of culture) but too little theory'[4] but a tradition also divided to the point of antagonism over this relation between culture and social structure.

The British social anthropologists tend to think of themselves as sociologists concerned primarily with the social structures and institutions of primitive societies, or they utilize social structure as a frame for the organization and interpretation of cultural phenomena; most American ethnologists consider culture as the major concept and point of departure and subordinate social structure to it, if they utilize this concept at all, preferring to operate with concepts of culture pattern and culture form.[5]

Let us take a journey through the history and development of anthropology to address the origins of some of these definitions and antagonisms.

It would be hard to overestimate the impact that Darwin's theory of evolution had upon thought and belief in modern western society during the latter part of the nineteenth century, and, indeed, the influence that it has continued to exercise up until the present day. The implications of Darwin's thesis spilled rapidly out of the confines of zoological concerns with the adaptation of certain animal species to their particular habitats, and came into collision with Christian theology, over the explanation of human origins. The Church had maintained its power, or at least its moral sanction, over the populace, on the basis that humankind was the spontaneous and benevolent gift of an omnipotent Deity and as such should rightly remain subject to His control, through the mediating influence of religious institutions. Even though the successes and excesses of modern science had gone some considerable way towards the secularization of our understandings of natural processes, the question of origins still remained very much an issue of faith. What Darwin provided was an explosion of both the inner and outer horizons of human potential that was much more in line with the desires and achievements of modernity's project. The theory of evolution formulated the origin of the species 'homo sapiens' through a naturalistic reduction to former, and lesser, species of creature. This set a trail that natural science would continue to pursue, backwards, to the more and even more fundamental particles that constitute our physical being; with the biochemists' DNA of the 1960s becoming one major signpost. Perhaps more significantly – and particularly so in relation to the social and cultural sciences – the destruction of one set of mythologies concerning the beginnings of humankind gave rise to a new mythology concerning its purpose and its destiny. The theory of evolution provided a scientific justification for the ideologies of growth and development that had, once entangled with the capitalist enterprise, become equated with the 'good' of civilization. Darwin rendered these previously covert 'grand narratives' of modernity both visible and uncontestable. The 'thinking and achieving ape' was now clearly the measure of all things and the Enlightenment project was complete. The condition of modern (western) history was the best that could be; it was, after all, the pinnacle of human achievement.

This realization was utterly political in character (adhering to Lawson's[6] view that 'science is true because it is powerful, not powerful because it is true'). It established a rationale for colonialism, in excess of economic avarice; a fillip to the technological triumph of culture over nature, through the transformation of found-object into product; and the grounds for anthropology as a way of understanding the world.

The link between evolutionary theory and anthropology is very important to our contemporary thinking about culture. The original theorists in this field were, in fact, referred to as 'evolutionists', and were concerned to investigate the social origins of humankind. Their thoughts were directed to the Barbarians of Antiquity and beyond to the Savages who marked the start of social relations, as we now recognize them. The savage, of course, was an extinct breed but the 'evolutionists' found their convenient modern counterpart in the 'primitive' peoples that still populated the relatively distant and exotic parts of the world, like central Africa, South America and inland Australia.

It was the American anthropologist Lewis Henry Morgan (1818–81) who produced and elaborated the first hierarchical classificatory scales of human evolutionary civilization. There is no sense in which his schemes can be understood as descriptive morphologies. They are clearly judgemental, and on moral and ethnocentric bases. The continua of human types that he provides are based on a deeply held sense of differential achievement, or what we have come to know as 'evolutionary stages'. These stages he actually describes as statuses, ranging from the 'lower status of savagery' up to the 'status of civilization', all based on the society's means of subsistence. For Morgan the historical process became understood as a linear competition, between alternatively situated groups of people, in which human beings match their innate abilities against the various constraints of their environments. Thus combinations of race and scarce resources give rise to the distributions of modern peoples and their relative levels of civilization.

The latest investigations respecting the early condition of

the human race, are tending to the conclusion that mankind commenced their career at the bottom of the scale and worked their way up from savagery to civilization through the slow accumulations of experimental knowledge.

As it is undeniable that portions of the human family have existed in a state of savagery, other portions in a state of barbarism, and still other portions in a state of civilization, it seems equally so that these three distinct conditions are connected with each other in a natural as well as necessary sequence of progress. Moreover, that the status attained by each branch respectively, is rendered probable by the conditions under which all progress occurs and by the known advancement of several branches of the family through two or more of these conditions.[7]

Morgan's works have, through the ironies of modern interpretation, come to be seen as an influence on Karl Marx and the development of modern socialism but also as an apologia for the development of capitalism. His comparative ethnology in no way implies his personal indifference or antagonism towards what he might have designated as 'less advanced people'; he was, in fact, an active philanthropist and campaigner on behalf of the American Indians; but it did provide an authoritative basis for such thinking which is still recognizable within the modern complex and confusions over racism, racial superiority, development and underdevelopment, the politics of the third world, and even arguments concerning the relative merits of 'high' as opposed to 'low' culture.

Morgan, although working with an implicit concept of the collective, and methodologically comparative, way of life of a people, never realized this as a definition of culture. He had established a model for the anthropological analysis of culture in relation to social structure, but the work of clarifying and refining the concept of 'culture' itself was to be left to future scholars. Contemporary with Morgan, but foundational of the English school of social anthropology at Oxford University, was Edward Burnett Tylor (1832–1917), a theorist also recognizable as an 'early evolutionist'. It is generally agreed that the original definition of culture, within anthropology, was provided by Tylor. He informs us that 'Culture or Civilization, taken in its wide ethnographic sense, is that complex whole which includes knowledge, belief, art, morals, law, custom, and any other capabilities and habits acquired by man as a member of society'.[8] This definition is critical in understanding the relationship between culture and social structure because it does not distinguish social organization and social institutions from a general concept of culture. Such a view sets the pattern for a tradition of cultural criticism and appreciation based on very different premises to the philosophical views of Kant and the literary stance adopted by Wordsworth, Coleridge, Carlyle and Arnold. These competitive versions of culture find contemporary review in the works of Williams and Hoggart, and remain a constant preoccupation of this text.

Tylor, in common with many subsequent anthropologists, was preoccupied with the character and content of human belief systems. However, unlike many of his contemporaries, he did not suppose that religious belief was the sole prerogative of 'advanced', non-primitive people. Although he held to strict evolutionist views concerning the differential quality and levels of achievement embodied in the cultural representations of different groups of people, he categorically asserted that religion, or a 'belief in Spiritual beings', was common to all human thinking. The savage mind, like that of a modern person, is confronted with the anxiety concerning mortality and the mysteries presented through reverie; we all resolve such conundrums through a notion of the soul. It may be that the primitive confuses spirits with realities, blurs subjectivity with objectivity, and allows a proliferation of deities intolerable to a sophisticated monotheism, but all humankind understands through the capacity for religious symbolism. We can now add to this thesis the views of James Frazer concerning primitive thought. Frazer in his major anthropological, yet highly literary, work The Golden Bough (1890), addressed primitive knowledge, cosmology and forms of explanation. He generated the remarkable conclusion that magic is, in effect, a proto-scientific epistemology based on mistaken principles concerning the relationship between events.

Between them, the 'early evolutionists', Morgan, Tylor and Frazer, generated certain fundamental propositions concerning the nature of homo sapiens, as a social being, that are formative in our discussion of the relation between culture and social structure. Above all they provide us with the view that all human history is unified, it follows a common route, a grand human tradition. Informing this is the absolute belief in the universal structure of human consciousness; what we might call the psychic unity of the human species. And finally they indicate that the concepts of culture and civilization are continuous. These are the three guiding and explanatory axioms of early anthropology which, as I shall now show, waned during the subsequent paradigm of social scientific knowledge, but re-emerged during the 1950s under the auspices of Claude Lévi-Strauss, fashionably disguised as 'structuralism' and thus more appropriately linked to the modern engagement with the linguistic character of cultural formations.

The understanding of culture within the social sciences now moved in a direction quite contrary to the basic premises of 'evolutionism'. A new mood was afoot; colonialism, though still rife as a feature of international relations, was coming to be understood as a political rather than a patrician act. Now there was a spectrum of liberalism which had, for some while, tempered the traditional political systems of western states largely because of its beneficial contributions to the functioning of modern capitalist economies. This liberalism had extended into the doctrines of socialism, with its concerns over justice and equality. While retaining a respect for difference, perhaps through the influence of Karl Marx, powerful ideas about history had emerged disentangling it from 'natural progress' or 'evolution' and linking it inextricably with material interests that were essentially human. Culture, then, came to be seen not as a sequential manifestation of an inevitably unfolding saga, extending from savagery to the heights of civilization, but rather as what people collectively 'do' in their different ways, in different places and at different times.

Cultures came to be understood as historically particular, and the relations between different cultures became a matter of inductive generalization rather than deductive reductionism. To put this another way, we might say that, in relation to cultural criticism and appraisal, the dominant paradigm of 'evolutionism', which necessarily rested on *absolutist* beliefs, was replaced by one of 'historicalism' based on a commitment to *relativism*. This swing to relativism, an espousal of the particularity and situation-specific meaning of all aspects of culture and social action, was to dominate anthropology and sociology for at least the next half-century, and is, in fact, still current in the modern academy's political preference for pluralism and difference.

In the context of this next, significant, step forward in the understanding of the collective lives of people by social scientists, 'culture' continued to be used as a general, overarching term rather than a concept referring to a specialized or elite segment of their activity or symbolic repertoire. Boas in America, and, latterly, Malinowski and Radcliffe-Brown in England, strengthened anthropology's commitment to culture being understood as a way of life, but their sense differs from Tylor's original views in their insistence and sustained emphasis on the plurality of cultures as being isolated, discrete, independently functioning, integrally organized totalities; and also in their shift from an attachment to the notion of evolution running through human relations.

What cultural unities might exist could now only be constructed with the aid of the elaborate mosaic of data gradually being accumulated from numerous, exhaustive, and often repetitive ethnographies. Ethnography, or 'fieldwork', rather than 'grand theory', was to set the pattern for much subsequent anthropology and was, indeed, destined to re-emerge as the avant-garde model for methodology in both sociology and cultural studies in the 1980s. This development – which (in its original form) American anthropology knows as the 'Boas Revolution' – instanced, among other things, a move to an empirically grounded rather than a universal theory of explanation. It also reveals a quantum leap in the politics of social science's claims for veracity: a modest and self-effacing retreat from speculative universalism to a new faith in the accuracy and ruthless honesty of face-to-face encounters. Finally, we might suggest that it shows an affirmation of the belief in the self-sustaining 'goodness' of difference; which finds a further contemporary resonance in the invocation of 'community' as a unit of action by the modern-day social services.

During what we might call its 'relativism' period, anthropology, though concerted in one sense, began to fragment in other ways. It lived within, but did not devote itself entirely to, the Tylorian concept of culture. Radcliffe-Brown developed 'social anthropology', a powerful subdiscipline, which engaged in the comparative study of 'social structure', a concept deriving from Durkheim, which, as we have discussed, pointed to the externality, typicality and constraining influence of particular formations contained within the collective consciousness of a people, that compelled them to act routinely in certain integrative and solidaristic ways. At the same time Boas, the true father of

American anthropology, and Malinowski in England were extending the existing ethnology and developing cultural anthropology which studies cultures more in terms of ideas, symbols and artefacts. Both theorists also emphasized comparative and historical perspectives.

A significant division, within the new paradigm of historicalism and relativism in the understanding of cultures, emerged initially as a result of the competition between W. H. R. Rivers, who was Radcliffe-Brown's tutor and mentor, and A. L. Kroeber, Boas's protégé, over the appropriate interpretation of Morgan's analytic distinction between classificatory and descriptive kinship systems. This seemingly arcane debate gave rise to the two rival anthropological theories of culture that were to set the character of the discipline(s) and establish the identity of their followers almost up until the present day. The two analytic protagonists were the theory of 'culture patterns', following the inspirations of Alfred Kroeber, and the theory of 'social structure', which was very much the position propounded by Rivers, Radcliffe-Brown and his followers. The division institutionalized, in this country, into a long and continuing debate between Malinowski as the progenitor of cultural anthropology and Radcliffe-Brown as the figurehead of the new social anthropology. The debate even came to symbolize the difference between anthropology and sociology, a disciplinary distinction which has today eroded analytically, only to be re-established substantively in terms of the axis pre-industrial/industrial.

THE PATTERN THEORY OF CULTURE

The gospel for this approach was generated by Kroeber and Kluckhohn who provided an exhaustive, and exhausting, review and partial analysis of myriad existing definitions and formulations of the concept of culture in an attempt to distil a productive synthesis:

> Culture consists of patterns, explicit and implicit, of and for behaviour, acquired and transmitted by symbols, constituting the distinctive achievement of human groups, including their embodiments in artifacts; the essential core of culture consists of traditional (i.e. historically derived and selected) ideas and especially their attached values; culture systems may, on the one hand, be con-

sidered as products of action, on the other as conditioning elements of further action.[9]

There is no doubt that this formulation was an advance on a prevalent behaviourist, reductionist view that culture was comprised of learned behaviour. Kroeber and Kluckholn continue:

> . . . culture is not behaviour nor the investigation of behaviour in all its concrete completeness. Part of culture consists in norms for or standards of behaviour. Still another part consists of ideologies justifying or rationalizing certain selected ways of behaviour. Finally, every culture includes broad general principles of selectivity and ordering ('highest common factors') in terms of which patterns of and for and about behaviour in very varied areas of culture content are reducible to parsimonious generalization.[10]

The 'pattern theory of culture', which was also to be seen in the works of Sapir, Benedict, White, Bateson and others, argues for the general and recurrent elements of culture to be understood apart from social structure; thus it recommends the study of patterns, form, structure and organization in culture rather than discrete cultural traits and culture content: '. . . how patterns of art, religion, philosophy, as well as of technology and science, waxed and waned, acquired their characteristic content and kept rolling majestically along, quite independently of particular individuals'.[11]

Such a thesis is not ignoring the issue of social structure but regards such deep structural patterns of social organization as entrenched and less amenable to transformation. All levels of culture are treated as subject to patterning but not all to the same degree or to the same stage of conscious awareness. Fashion was one configuration within culture of which Kroeber produced an analysis, and which has an obvious application to the theory in terms of its modishness. Pattern then was an abstraction that enabled the theorist to attend to the commonality of all elements of a culture, while also attending to their particularity in terms of their persistence and complexity. It also allows for an emergence of cultural symbolism not determined semiotically by the constraints of biological nature, the physical environment or a static and compelling version of social structure. The theory enables a coherent movement from religion to diet, from politics to dress, and from mode of production to artefact. The rolling, historical 'superorganicism' of Kroeber reduces the role of the individual to that of being the instrument of culture or the vehicle of patterning; here the essentialism is that of the cultural rather than the social structural: 'The social or cultural . . . is in very essence non-individual. Civilization, as such, begins only where the individual ends.'[12]

Unlike traditional sociological explanation, pattern theory does not generate hypotheses beginning with the energizing social structure. In fact pattern theory tends to avoid causal explanations altogether. Its topic, and hypothesis, is a complex network of patterning, through history, which defies a finite starting point.

SOCIAL STRUCTURE AS A THEORY OF CULTURE

For all of the advances brought about through the 'Boas Revolution' in anthropological thought, its commitment to 'particularity' and its consequent jackdaw-like obsession with the accumulation of ethnographic field data led to a gap in theory. The celebration of and luxuriation in the rich differences that cultural variability provides left anthropology vulnerable to the predation of an all-encompassing theoretical framework. This was provided by British social anthropology in the form of *functionalism*, a grand and comprehensive perspective that was to monopolize sociological and anthropological thought for several decades up until the 1960s. Functionalism's guiding analytic principles were 'integration' and 'interrelation' and as such culture and social structure came to be viewed as identical, or at least continuous.

> This brings us to a fundamental axiom of the science of society, as I see it. Is a science of culture possible? Boas says it is not. I agree. You cannot have a science of culture. You can study culture only as a characteristic of a social system. Therefore, if you are going to have a science, it must be a science of social systems.[13]

Radcliffe-Brown was the dominant figure in this significant conceptual development. His theory derived from Durkheim (indeed, it was his interpretation that established Durkheim's misplaced reputation as a 'naughty' functionalist), particularly the early Durkheim, and suffered from an overdeveloped adherence to the 'organic' analogy with the methodological consequences of

a comparative social morphology dedicated to the rigid classification of different social structural *species* and *genera*, and a
social physiology concerned with accounting for their 'normal',
as opposed to pathological, functioning.

> For the further elaboration of the concept [function] it is
> convenient to use the analogy between social life and
> organic life. . . . The system of relations by which these
> units are related is the organic structure. As the term is
> here used, the organism is not itself the structure, it is a
> collection of units arranged in a structure, i.e., in a set
> of relations. . . . As the word function is here being used,
> the life of the organism is conceived as the functioning
> of its structure. It is through and by the continuity of
> the functioning that the continuity of the structure is
> preserved. . . . To turn from organic life to social life, if
> we examine such a community as an African or Austra-
> lian tribe, we can recognize the existence of a social
> structure. Individual human beings, the essential units in
> this instance, are connected by a definite set of social
> relations into an integrated whole. The continuity of the
> social structure, like that of an organic structure is not
> destroyed by changes in the units. . . . The continuity is
> maintained by the process of social life, which consists
> of the activities and interactions of individual human
> beings and of organized groups into which they are
> united. The social life of a community is here defined as
> the functioning of the social structure.[14]

It is not hard to imagine why the organic analogy is not in current
use in the social sciences; its exponents, like Herbert Spencer,
seemed more concerned to preserve the model rather than
employ it as a source of explanation. However, Radcliffe-Brown
uses it rigorously in order to justify the application of the concept
of 'function' in his analyses. Radcliffe-Brown produced a theory
of social structure which he saw as a network of social relations
including persistent social groups, social categories, classes and
social roles. It was assumed that each social structural system is
a self-sustaining, homeostatic, harmonious functional unit; hence
the primacy of interrelatedness. Empirically the work attests to
this by examining always the parts, not as they exist in their
own right, but rather as they function in relation to the whole.
Interrelations and functional interdependence are keys to such

analysis. Another major strand to such work is the study of evolutionary structural change, not radical or revolutionary change but the gradual and predictable transformation of one form into another. This is both historical and archaeological, but essentially morphological. Radcliffe-Brown's theory of social structure, which is also an inclusive theory of culture, is taken to be universal in its application. Here is a framework requiring no modification when directed towards an understanding of all and any culture both across space and through time.

Radcliffe-Brown and his followers dispensed with the concept of culture in their accounts, and also denied that the term referred to an autonomous realm partly on the territorial grounds that their work addressed the only social reality, namely, social structures. This was, however, somewhat disingenuous as their concept also implicitly embraces a strong sense of culture. So for example, Meyer Fortes writes that social structure is not just 'an aspect of culture but an entire culture of a given people handled in a special frame of theory'.[15] Nevertheless, the consequence of this posturing was that Radcliffe-Brown is remembered not for his contribution to a theory of culture but rather as the progenitor of an influential social theory which defined the explanatory concept 'function' solely in relation to the abstraction 'social structure', hence its designation as 'structural-functionalism'.

MALINOWSKI AND CULTURAL ANTHROPOLOGY

Malinowski is deserving of a section of his own because he eludes my theoretic categories for organizing the anthropological tradition, that is to say his designations are almost completely transgressive. He was a Polish natural scientist who went on to hold a British chair in anthropology contemporary with that of Radcliffe-Brown, espoused functionalism, and yet clearly delineated culture as distinct from social structure, and thus formed a school of 'cultural' as opposed to 'social' anthropology sharing many of the concerns of the American tradition.

Malinowski's functionalism was based in the needs of the individual rather than in those of the social system. So when he specifies that culture is made up of the 'seven basic human needs' they are factors like nutrition, reproduction, comfort and safety, all located in the individual consciousness rather than that of the group or wider collectivity; they do, nevertheless, contribute in concert to the integration of the whole society. This individualization of cultural response and generation is the kernel of his different perspective and the breakpoint of his functionalism from structural-functionalism.

> Professor Radcliffe-Brown is, as far as I can see, still developing and deepening the views of the French socio-logical school. He thus has to neglect the individual and disregard biology.
>
> Functionalism differs from other sociological theories more definitely, perhaps, in its conception and definition of the individual than in any other respect. The func-tionalist includes in his analysis not merely the emotional as well as intellectual side of mental processes, but also insists that man in his full biological reality has to be drawn into our analysis of culture. The bodily needs and environmental influences, and the cultural relation to them, have to be studied side by side.[16]

Malinowski often referred to culture as 'the social heritage' and revealed a conceptualization closer to that of the English literary tradition than to the more universalist view of, say, Tylor. He did, like Radcliffe-Brown, retain a not-too-deep-seated evolution-ism and an articulate sense of cultural superiority. Beyond these considerations in his approach to culture he believed strongly in the necessity of detailed fieldwork and encouraged study on the interface between disciplines, such as sociology, psychology, his-tory and anthropology.

A further dimension of analysis emerges again here. What-ever the textual differentiation of content, of 'culture' versus 'social structure', that occurred within the theoretical hegemony of British functionalism(s), they shared a conception of time. This temporal dimension is critical in the study of culture, today as then. Functionalism, through its dependence on stasis, has no practical or theoretical relationship with change. The topic of study is the 'organism', or the functioning totality, held in time through the balance of its 'internal' mechanisms of interdepen-dency and interrelation. This is what contemporary structuralism has taught us to refer to as 'synchronicity'. Such a temporal commitment inevitably places limitations upon the phenomenon. Functionalist anthropology restricted itself, by and large, to the study of contemporary non-literate societies. It could not attach itself to their past or to societies that had died out. Such work was left to subsequent developments in the discipline, such as those by Evans-Pritchard who brought in materials from history and archaeology, investigated the tradition of reason in the primitive mind, the social constraints of memory and, in common with modern-day ethnomethodology, the significance of accounting procedures in everyday understandings.

> It is . . . a mistake to say that savages perceive mystically or that their perception is mystical. On the other hand we may say that savages pay attention to phenomena on account of the mystical properties with which their society has endowed them, and that often their interest in phenomena is mainly, even exclusively, due to these mystical properties.[17]

Subsequently anthropologists such as Firth began to study the same society but at different time periods and develop ideas of 'accumulation', 'inheritance' and 'transmission'.

> If . . . society is taken to be an organized set of individuals with a given way of life, culture is that way of life. If society is taken to be an aggregate of social relations, then culture is the content of those relations. Society emphasises the human component, the aggregate of people and the relations between them. Culture emphasises the component of accumulated resources, immaterial as well as material, which the people inherit, employ, transmute, add to and transmit.[18]

Beyond this the newer generations of anthropologist risked the centrality of stability and order in their theory by studying conflict within simple societies. Other studies were directed at rural and peasant societies in the modern-day and even modern, urban, non-primitive communities. Such recent initiatives into the realm of the 'diachronic', the study of phenomena through time, dissociated anthropology from its seemingly fixed relationship with isolated primitive cultures. The phenomenon under study now becomes increasingly complex: if it is not an issue of geography or stability or primitiveness then what constitutes the identity and difference of each and any culture? This is a problem not just for anthropology but for the sociology of culture and for 'cultural studies'. What constitutes the boundaries of culture? Much modern work would appear to treat 'pop culture', 'youth subculture', 'East End culture', 'Azande culture' and perhaps even 'postmodern culture' with an equivalence. We might suggest that their differences reside in a conception of social structure.

NOTES

[1] E. Durkheim and M. Mauss, *Primitive Classification*, London: Routledge & Kegan Paul (1970).

[2] B. Bernstein, *Class, Codes and Control* Vols 1, 2 and 3, London: Routledge & Kegan Paul (1971–3); G. Alexander (ed.), *Durkheimian Sociology: Cultural Studies*, Cambridge: Cambridge University Press (1988).

[3] T. Parsons, *The Social System*, London: Routledge & Kegan Paul (1951).

[4] A. L. Kroeber and C. Kluckholn (1952), *Culture: A Critical Review of Concepts and Definitions*, New York: Vintage Books (1963).

[5] F. Eggan, *Social Anthropology of North American Tribes*, Chicago: University of Chicago Press (1955), p. 490.

[6] H. Lawson, *Reflexivity: The Postmodern Predicament*, London: Hutchinson (1985).

[7] L. H. Morgan, *Ancient Society* (1877), p. 3.

[8] E. B. Tylor (1871), *Primitive Culture: Researches into the Development of Mythology, Philosophy, Religion, Art and Custom*, Gloucester, MA: Smith (1958), p. 1.

[9] A. L. Kroeber and C. Kluckholn, op. cit., p. 181.

[10] Ibid., p. 189.

[11] M. Harris, *The Rise of Anthropological Theory*, New York: Thomas Y. Crowell (1968), p. 328.

[12] A. Kroeber, 'The superorganic', *American Anthropologist* Vol. XIX, 1917, p. 192.

[13] A. R. Radcliffe-Brown, *A Natural Science of Society*, Glencoe, IL: Free Press (1957), p. 106.

[14] A. R. Radcliffe-Brown, *Structure and Function in Primitive Society*, Cambridge: Cambridge University Press (1952), p. 176.

[15] M. Fortes, 'The structure of unilineal descent groups', *American Anthropologist* New Series 55, 1953, pp. 17–51.

[16] B. Malinowski, 'Review of six essays on culture by Albert Blumenthal', *American Sociological Review* Vol. 4, 1939, p. 939.

[17] E. Evans-Pritchard, 'Levy-Bruhl's theory of primitive mentality', *Bulletin of the Faculty of Arts* (Cairo) II, p. 29.
[18] R. Firth, *Elements of Social Organization*, London: Watts (1951).

3

Culture and social action

Max Weber, a leading theorist of modernity, may be constructively viewed as a culminating figure in a lineage of nineteenth-century German social analysts. This school of thinkers, including such eminent figures as Ranke, Dilthey and Rickert – the latter being a contemporary of Weber – have come to be referred to as the Heidelberg 'cultural philosophers' and were all, in their various ways, contributing to the debate concerning the constitution and epistemological status of cultural phenomena. To this end their legacy has made a considerable contribution to our contemporary thinking about the cultural realm, one which has some continuities with the English literary tradition, already discussed, but one which is also utterly opposed to the once predominant anthropological sense of social structure, previously considered. This body of ideas proceeds from a strong sense of the a priori, that which is intrinsic to and universal within the human condition.

The cultural philosophers were all working within a set of problematics that find their roots in the overshadowing, yet inspirational, presence of the philosopher Kant. Kant, it may be recalled, had, by a different root, exercised a considerable influence on the aesthetics of Coleridge. However, within the German academy Kant was no casual or accidental presence. It would be fairer to say that his ideas grounded all intellectual discourse such that much thinking in his wake has been designated 'neo-Kantian', including that of Weber. Given the combative state of knowledge through and up to the turn of the century, Weber's tradition is conventionally regarded as being engaged in the epistemological struggle or, to put it at its least contentious, the tension between the knowledge claims of idealism and positivism.

Kantian philosophy established and projected the twin, seemingly irreconcilable, concerns of 'morality' and 'science'. These two fundamental elements were suggestive of different realms of existence embodying mutually exclusive conceptions of humankind; on the one hand the pure, ideal creature and on the other the embodied, practical being. This radical dualism in Kant's thinking is perpetually manifested in the severance between the 'mind' and the 'body'. The mind makes reference to the spiritual character of human existence; this is a major formulation of the *Geist* of all German idealist philosophy which reaches fruition in Hegel's transcendental rationalism. The body signifies the natural character of human existence, thus constitutes the concrete, factual source of humankind's empirical being in the world, and, in turn, provides the material inspiration for positivist philosophies. This dualism in Kant is refashioned by the cultural philosophers, Weber included, in terms of the clear distinctions that they draw between the understandings of the 'cultural sciences' and the 'natural sciences', respectively.

This distinction, this major problematic, is set within the context of a further Kantian conceptualization, that is, the notion of 'synthetic a priori truths'. This building block in Kant's philosophical system is referring to statements about the world that are universally and necessarily true (in this sense they are a priori); however, the necessity of such truths cannot be derived from an analysis of the meanings of such truths (in this sense they are synthetic). They are not merely logical deductions or principles, they tell us something 'additional' about the world. Classic philosophical examples would be statements such as 'all events have causes' and 'a thing cannot be two colours at the same time'. For Kant there are two sources of such knowledge, and these have a significant bearing upon the discussion of Weber's cultural sociology, which is to follow. These two sources are firstly *sensibility*, which is an intuition of the immanent forms of being, and secondly *understanding*, which points us to the application of appropriate categories of thought, like space, time and causality. In sequence we can see these sources as heralding Weber's idea of *Verstehen* and his ideal-type constructs.

In the broadest terms then, following Kant, the cultural philosophers viewed the individual actor as a free moral agent not appropriately subject to analysis by the generalizing methods of the natural sciences. The epistemological work of Weber and his forebears thus became the clarification of the systematic yet socially constructed character of the concepts of cultural science and the grounding of their construction in the notions of difference and value.

How would we summarize Weber's contribution to our understanding of culture? How useful is Weber's method as yet another implement for our contemporary work? Yet prior to this we need perhaps ask, to what problem, as Weber saw it, does his cultural scientific methodology provide a solution? It is reasonable to assert that, according to a variety of sources (including the biography by his wife), Weber had no grandiose methodological aspirations. He wrote his now highly regarded essays on methodology[1] at a stage of his life that concluded a sustained period of conceptual confusion, non-productivity and psychological disturbance and he regarded them as an act of purification, or perhaps, rather, clarification, of the massive corpus of research and writing that had proceeded this hiatus. To this degree he was unlike Durkheim in his desire to form a School of sociological technique and practice. Weber really wanted to make clear for others what he thought was the timeless and inevitable strategy for understanding socio-cultural phenomena. Nevertheless, his views provided a justification for a shift in the activities of the cultural sciences and an announcement of their special identity. It did so, in part, by providing a critique of certain classical economic theorists (a tactic also employed by Karl Marx) such as Roscher and Knies. In this sense the methodology essays are utterly pragmatic; they were, for Weber, a means rather than an end. In line with his obsessive and consuming passion for gaining knowledge about the history and culture of human collectivities, Weber's methodological canons actually enabled or facilitated further research, they did not specify its absolute character. In this light it has been reasonably asserted by Burger[2] that in many ways Weber's methodological ideas are not very original; rather they belong to the intellectual conventions of the previous cultural philosophers. Weber's concern with the logical status of concepts is quite clearly based on the work of Rickert[3] whom he openly acknowledged. However, the modern 'mystery story' that we call the ideal type and his ideas concerning value-neutrality are both original formulations in our analyses of cultural formations. Weber's method of cultural analysis proceeded from certain strongly held views on the nature of social enquiry. He asserted that cultural knowledge should be conceptual in character rather than descriptive and an attempt at literal representation. This distanced him from his early mentor Ranke who had stated that it is the 'business of the historian to render the past in all its concrete detail'. Weber wished to locate cultural facticities within the realm of reason, the exercise of mind, the course of action that is uniquely human. Beyond this it is well rehearsed that Weber sought to resist the intrusion of judgements of value into the rigorous practice of his social science; which is not to say that Weber failed to recognize the infinitely value-laden character of cultural phenomena themselves, nor was he unaware of the value-laden character of the rejection of values. Culture is the practice of humankind, as is its understanding. Finally he resisted the compelling idea, that stemmed from the obvious and apparent success of the natural sciences, that social, historical or cultural analysis should aspire to the establishment of laws and empirical generalizations. The neo-Kantians held to the view that within the cultural realm of phenomena no essence or noumenal form could be revealed, only appearances or phenomenal forms were available and thus the search for laws relating the existence of essences was unjustifiable. This means that cultural science is different from, but not inferior to, the natural sciences. Rather, the former is challenging to the latter. All scientific activity must seek to produce a knowledge that is objective but they do so by capturing phenomena through their different modes of discourse. Simply stated, both natural and cultural sciences generate realities through their processes of abstraction, so the different character of their realities belongs to the differences in their processes, or methods. Objective knowledge is socially contexted and would thus be varied; it belongs to the shared rules of agreement within a group of scientists (or cultural theorists). This resonates with Kuhn's[4] notion of paradigmatic knowledge.

Knowledge, for the cultural philosophers, was always a state of mind, it was not a correspondential copy of reality – whatever that might be. Culture can thus be treated not as a deposition, or a reflection, or a superstructural representation of a material state; it is autonomous, as it is a course of action. Cultural phenomena have a content that emerges through human intention; certain sensations or impressions are given to us through the character of our relation to the world. We then place a form upon them by imposing a category of thought or an idea upon them. Thus 'facts' emerge as a confluence of sensation and significance, and they assume the status of a segment, singled out and held from the undifferentiated mass of reality. Facts, as the elementary simples of knowing, are thus constituted in the mind. They are intentional acts not constant features of an orderly universe. Experience is potentially limitless or infinite, that is, the universe is continuous in its unavailability. Confronting this, the human mind is finite. The action of knowing thus saves the universe from its randomness.

Methodology, for Weber, within the social and cultural sciences, is an adherence to consensus principles of selection and abstraction. Without a sustained, consistent methodology subjective knowledges would proliferate because of the idiosyncratic nature of human difference. Seen in this way, objectivity for the cultural sciences becomes not the establishment of the absolute 'correct' facts but the reflexive assurance of the selection of the same facts for all practitioners. Objective knowledge is, therefore, intersubjective, it is part of a social context, as always is its object of concern.

The distinction that Weber and the cultural philosophers draw between 'natural' and 'cultural' sciences is based on the logical status of the concepts with which the different spheres of understanding operate. Human beings overcome the burden of infinity through the selection of facts, and the different criteria employed in the selection of facts signify the location of the understanding as being either 'natural' or 'cultural'. So the selection of the common elements of events gives rise to the *general* concepts of the 'natural' sciences (these are the concepts that ignore individual difference), and the selection of the unique elements of events gives rise to the *individual*, the particular concepts of the 'cultural sciences'.

Both Rickert and Weber accept the validity and efficacy of the laws of nature that are elucidated through the natural sciences but hold the reservation that they do not exhaust all that we need to know. This is in large part due to the fact that they are essentially material, they are static and they presume determinacy. In relation to cultural phenomena they would abuse the volatile and emergent qualities of such socially and historically contexted processes and events. The work of the cultural philosophers is thus in favour of individual, particularistic concepts, ideas which speak of intentionality and autonomy, and place culture firmly in the sphere of action. I shall demonstrate this point in a moment in connection with Weber's thesis on the origins and growth of modern capitalism, but at this stage we may usefully pursue his methodology of cultural analysis.

A clear threat to any method that seems to espouse a particularistic individualism is that it lays itself open to a proliferation of subjective relativisms – what is there to prevent the emergence of as many accounts of a phenomena as there are theorists producing the accounts? Well, in one sense, nothing at all. However, knowing, like other social and cultural phenomena (which for Weber's purposes are his topic) is also a collective course of action constrained by convention, tradition, reason and morality. There is a collective consciousness, or perhaps a complex intersubjectivity, which applies to knowing as to all courses of action. Thus, the way in which cultural theorists will make discriminations between things is located in space and time; it will make reference to general cultural values which are the contemporary practical evaluations embedded in the social institutions that constitute the structure of the epoch. This is a truly sociological point. Secondly, cultural analysis escapes relativism by assessing its topic not in terms of utterly private and idiosyncratic values, but rather in terms of historically relevant values. This idea of value relevance is sometimes treated by commentators on Weber as an exercise in empathy. In this way cultural knowledge, for Weber, can be scientific because it is rigorously and reflexively constructed, but it is always a mental image (an intention, a 'metaphor' almost) rather than a copy of reality. Cultural phenomena are constructed in thought; empirical data are mastered through the imposition of value – but this is the delicate interpretive work of *Verstehen* not the mechanical grasping, collecting and replicating of *Begreifen* that typifies the methods of positivism and the natural sciences. For Weber, then, cultural phenomena are constituted through human values and their understanding further requires the imposition of judgements of value. So when Weber tells us that 'in action is included all human behaviour in so far as the actor attaches a subjective meaning to it' he is referring to the individual members of society doing what is intended or purposive rather than that which is instinctual or reactive, but he is also referring to the practice of the other members of their society (perhaps the theorist of culture) in placing a meaning upon an action to render it meaningful and coherent rather than nonsensical and random. This latter activity of making sense of others, Weber crystallizes in terms of his methodological concept of the 'ideal type'. The 'ideal type', as a device employed in the interpretation of culture, involves the analyst's projection of typical values and motivations into the supposed 'inner states' of the actors under scrutiny. But, of course, there is more to the 'ideal type' than this. Despite Weber's protestations concerning the non-originality, the taken-for-grantedness and the almost 'natural' character of 'ideal typing' as a way of understanding collective human conduct the idea remains elusive and confounding of generations of students of socio-cultural life.

Weber was using the 'ideal type' as a way of resolving the contradictory demands of idealism and positivism, and the alternative forms of explanation in terms of particularity or generality. Because of the essential dimension of subjectivity in the act of making sense, Weber recognized that the *individuality* of cultural concepts derived from the unique pattern in which the elements comprising the phenomenon occurred. He then attended to the issue that despite the uniqueness of each particular account of an aspect of culture, the definitional characteristics or the basic elements of such phenomena appear constant – although in each particular instance they are present in different degrees (so when we say 'capitalism', and perhaps imply slightly different things, we still all know what is being talked about). This recognition leads directly to the formation of the 'ideal type'. The 'ideal type' can be seen as an attempt to introduce a collective, comparative element into cultural analysis. The concept endeavours to solve the methodological problem of aspiring towards cultural 'generalizations' without the introduction of the *general* concepts characteristic of the natural sciences. It clarifies the relation between universal laws and historical descriptions, and helps to establish the epistemological status of the latter. Weber distils the essence of the 'ideal type' concept in four, often cited, passages from the *Methodology of the Social Sciences*:

The term ideal-typical is applied to categorizations of and statements about, relations between actors and action elements in terms of, or by reference to, the presence of one or a few maxims in the minds of actors according to which they orient their thoughts and actions.

An ideal type is formed by the one-sided exaggeration of one or several viewpoints and by the combination of a great many single phenomena existing diffusely and discretely, more or less present and occasionally absent, which are compatible with those one-sidedly emphasized viewpoints, into an internally consistent thought-picture. In its conceptual purity this thought-picture cannot be found empirically anywhere in reality, it is a utopia . . . .

Ideal types are statements of general form asserting the existence of certain constellations of elements which are empirically only approximated by the instances of the class of phenomenon to which each type refers.

[The ideal type] . . . is a thought picture which is neither the historical reality (i.e. its content is not a complete reproduction of concrete reality) nor even perhaps the 'true' reality (i.e. it does not present, in an absolute sense, the 'essence' of reality), whose purpose is even less to serve as a schema in which a part of reality should find its place as an instance (i.e. it is not a true general concept) but it has to be interpreted as a purely limiting concept for the comparison with and scrutiny of reality for the purpose of emphasizing certain significant parts of empirical reality.[5]

From these dense and often convoluted definitions we may elicit that the ideal type is essentially an heuristic device, a conceptual aid to thinking which certainly does not seek to exhaust its phenomenon. It is in no sense an hypothesis (though it may have some role in hypothesis formation) which would be the original proposition in a path of enquiry, and it does not serve to extract the lowest common denominators of an historical situation. So it is not an inductive generalization. Beyond this it relinquishes all claims to establishing an 'accurate' description of concrete reality. The 'ideal type' would seem to become defined in terms of what it is not. Rather than the 'ideal type' being comprised of an assembly of elements that are common to any particular empirical phenomenon it attempts to elucidate the 'significant' and 'charac- teristic' features of that phenomenon, that is, those features that

produce it as 'meaningful' and 'relevant' within its specific historical context. So, for example, Weber assembled the peculiar qualities of bureaucratic organization at the turn of the century in
terms of rationality and efficiency; a modern ideal type of
bureaucracy might seek to highlight dehumanization and inef-
ficiency. 'Ideal types' make reference to the autonomous symbolism of a phenomenon within a culture. The epistemological status
of an 'ideal type' is quite extraordinary; while it is made recognizable through an agglomeration of variables perceived differen-
tially within the empirical world, it is, actually, a fiction, an
imaginary leap, or what Weber chooses to call a utopia. Such a
utopia nevertheless has to fulfil certain criteria of plausibility: it
has to be internally coherent, and it must not defy common
sense.

All cultural phenomena, though often formidable in the constraint they exercise, are nevertheless fragile in that they are
generated and maintained by virtue of acting members of a
society placing and sustaining their own values within them. That
is to say that any cultural representation is contingent upon the
condition that it either reflects or embodies the ideas and interests
of the people to which it has any semiotic significance. The
state of a culture then makes reference to the shared individual
unconscious held by a people. This is a very diffuse concept but
it enables us to reconcile the multiplicity of possible meanings
that derive from how any particular aspect of culture appears to
different individuals and likewise the multiplicity of different
courses of action that may all contrive to give rise to a particular
aspect of culture. So social life and the understanding of social
life contain strategies (later to be considered under Garfinkel's
ethnomethodologies) which contrive to bring off a sense of uniformity and singularity in relation to our knowledge of cultural
events. We create types, typifications or ideal pictures, and
Weber's 'ideal type' is an attempt to regularize such a strategy
in the methodology of the cultural sciences. So when Weber
instructs us that we should create a 'one-sided exaggeration' he
is pointing to our calculated, reflexive disregard of the myriad
possible motives or inner-states of people that may have given
rise to an aspect of culture, and instead to act as if only a limited
number of possibilities were at work, and to see what stems from
an emphasis on those variables. An acceptance of this principle
allows for the non-contradictory possibility of having a proliferation of 'ideal types' concerning what common sense might regard

as the 'same' phenomenon. This is wholly appropriate for a cultural science where the different social theorists or historians work from within intellectual perspectives and value positions that are only ideologically exclusive. Furthermore, as different viewpoints are always emerging it is inappropriate to attempt to achieve an exhaustive system of 'ideal types'. Within this mood of quiet liberalism, however, it must be reiterated that these different viewpoints are not randomly arrived at, they make reference to the practical values in the mind of the particular theorist – so 'ideal types' are intended, they have a purpose within a committed value position.

The 'ideal type' may be seen as a device within a cultural science that operates at a level in excess of mere description, it is more general in character than utterly particular, but it is formulated in relation to an historical or cultural purpose. It is as if the method should catch the spirit of the social process, and perhaps no more than this could be claimed for it. Weber is adamant in his modesty when he affirms that 'the exact relation between the ideal type and empirical reality is problematic in every single case'. Although Parsons[6] accuses Weber of creating a 'mosaic atomism', a kind of collective assembly of essential reductions, this is itself an unjustifiable reduction. The 'ideal type' serves its purpose by parading and manifesting its unreality. Weber was concerned with understanding, the act of transformation; his contemporary controversy was with how a cultural science should abstract inductively from empirical reality. As an heuristic device the 'ideal type' seeks to get the work done, and it helps to provide working models, substantively based models, models that have a rigorous character.

Let us now turn to Weber's own ideal-typical analysis of the dominant culture of modernity, which he sees in the 'elective affinity' and mutual acceleration occurring between the Protestant ethic and the spirit of modern capitalism. This analysis is to be found in his major work[7] which many modern Marxist commentators, such as Zeitlin, Lewis and Hirst,[8] have read as an ideological justification and apologia for capitalism in the name of reason. This stems from a particular materialist view of human relations (that we shall consider in greater detail in the next chapter) which, although it assigns culture an active role in institutionalizing and legitimating the organization of society, tends to reduce this role to that of reproduction. Absent from the classical Marxist position, and central to Weber's, is an understanding of how culture not only sustains and reproduces social relationships, but also how it is instrumental in the production of the organizational forms of those relationships and the processes of their transformation through history. For Weber, culture is not reducible to the status of superstructure, that is, a reflection or expression of the underlying material structures, but is better understood as an autonomous basis of social order which is actively engaged in the practice of structuring social relationships in public and recognizable ways. Viewed from this position, and this is an important contribution to our modern understanding of the concept, culture has a logic of its own. It is in these terms, with culture being viewed as producer, as well as reproducer, of social relationships that Weber analyses the emergence and institutionalization of capitalism within western society as part of the rationalization of modernity, both in general and in particular. This is a point made forcibly by Walsh when he states that:

> What Weber points to, as being essentially noticeable, about modern capitalism is that it is a form of economic activity which is conducted in terms of a particular mentality which is essential to its nature. There is, then, a culture of capitalism – what Weber calls the Spirit of Capitalism – that is intrinsic to capitalist organisation and without which it cannot work as a form of economic activity.[9]

The 'Spirit' that Weber refers to is motivating and constraining, and yet intangible and not reducible to the notable set of emergent structural conditions such as the growth and centralization of commerce, the expansion of urbanization into cities, the dispossession of the peasantry from the land, the emergence of financial institutions and a social group to service them, and, most significantly, the growth and polarization of a system of stratification organized primarily around the issue of the ownership of the means of production. The Spirit of capitalism is not just a functional accompaniment to a burgeoning economic system which will map the destinies of generations to come, but, according to Marx, within a structure of social relations that is alienating, intolerable and constantly threatened by the fracturing of its contradictions. The Spirit of capitalism is operating at a different level. It is not just the legitimating buttress of a particular set of market relations, rather it provides a way of being that is both rational and moral, and also manifests itself at the level of individual psychology. Just as Durkheim had seen the integrative potential in a modern economic division of labour through a heterogeneous solidarity based on interdependence, so Weber sees the Spirit of capitalism not as producing a grand historical lie or distortion of the purpose of human species-being but instead he views it as producing a viable and all-embracing creed or purpose for being in the modern world. Entrepreneurs are driven to accumulate profit by a 'salvation anxiety' concerning their telos, and the working masses are driven to productivity by the self-affirming ethic of hard work (which 'never hurt anyone' and is good for the soul), the very purpose of being (a proposition agreed by Marx, outside of the conditions of exploitation).

This Spirit, the mentality of modernity, this shared set of values, establishes equilibrium at every level within the social system, despite the constant, and allegedly inherent fractures of the material base. Clearly, in Weber's view of culture, this *Zeitgeist* is imbued with both autonomy, and longevity. The rationality of modern capitalism, 'which rests on the expectation of profit by the utilisation of opportunities for exchange, that is, on formally peaceful chances of profit' is not simply the recommendation for a potentially Hobbesian war of each against all within a philosophy of avarice. It is part of a wider cultural complex that is held in check by an ethos of reciprocity of expectations based on honesty, frugality, punctuality and industriousness. This Protestant ethic, experienced by all as a 'calling', motivates honest labour as an expression of individual virtue and efficiency. The 'calling' is universal for Weber. As he says, it consists of 'an obligation which the individual is supposed to feel and does feel towards the content of his activity no matter in what it consists'.[10] The point of Weber's thesis is not, as some have supposed, to either justify the development of capitalism and its modes of stratification, nor to reduce an explanation of its development to the ascetic demands of certain branches of European non-conformist Protestantism. Rather, he is providing a persuasive basis for the understanding of dominant contemporary cultural formations in terms of the central efficacy, autonomy and generative force of ideas in action. Culture is immanent within human conduct and the patterns of action that emerge through its inter-subjectivity. Culture is never simply a reflection of pre-structured social relationships and the economic interests enshrined in them but, on the contrary, an agent in their production and maintenance. Weber has brought us further towards what Frisby and

Sayer[11] describe as 'society as an absent concept'. The socio-cultural realm is not a tangible material force, nor a reflection of such materiality; it resides in action, choice and value, all of which are subjective, intersubjective and volatile – but real, tangible and material in their consequences.

Culture as social action, an idea stemming in large part from Weberian thought, provides the ontological basis for a whole tradition of analysis within the social sciences; and one populated by a interesting diversity of bedfellows. The most obvious links between Weber's ideas and contemporary thought are provided for by the social phenomenologist Alfred Schutz, and also by the pre-eminent American sociologist Talcott Parsons, equally famous for his 'general theory of action' as he was for his 'social systems theory'.

SCHUTZ AND A SOCIAL PHENOMENOLOGY OF THE LIFE-WORLD

Schutz, born at the very end of the nineteenth century in Vienna, studied law and social theory and became preoccupied with the logic and methodology of the human sciences. He subsequently determined to establish a firm philosophical basis on which to interpret and accurately describe social interaction. It is within the finite provinces of meaning provided through interaction that culture becomes established and is reaffirmed. This is a culture without structural fixity and based on interpretation and 'multiple realities' emerging through social action; another firm instance of what we have described as a symbolic view of culture.

> . . . statements . . . of T. S. Eliot and . . . of Goethe, show the poet's insight into the fact that within a finite province of meaning of the work of art the interrelationship of the symbols as such is the essence of the poetic content and that it is unnecessary and may even be harmful to look for the referential scheme which the appresenting elements of the symbolic relationship would symbolize, if they were indeed objects of the world of everyday life. But their connection with these objects has been cut off; the use of the appresenting elements is just a means of communication; whereas poetry communicates by using ordinary language, the ideas symbolized

by this language are real entities within the finite province of meaning of poetical meaning.[12]

The single major influence on his work was the philosopher Husserl (also mentor to Heidegger), who introduced him to the 'science of the subjective', the new phenomenology, which was to provide a critique of the objectivism of all post-Socratic western philosophy. Husserl provided him with the three primary strands of his intellectual development through the theory of intentionality, his notion of intersubjectivity (which he incorporated with his reading of Weber), and the concept of the '*Lebenswelt*'. The conditions were set for Schutz to aspire to a grand reconciliation of Weber's 'sociology of *Verstehen*' and Husserl's 'transcendental phenomenology'. His work has endowed us in our approach to culture, first of all, with an attention to the centrality of consciousness; 'intentionality' affirming that consciousness is always consciousness of some thing, thus pointing to a dialectical theory of knowing, the provision of a sense of 'other' and, more significantly, to the constitutive practices of subjectivity through action. Secondly, Schutz centres his analysis not on the isolated subject, but on the meeting place between subjects, the cultural, the realm of intersubjectivity, which Weber had previously explored with his notions of choice, with his typologies of rational action and through his dictum that

> We shall speak of 'action' insofar as the acting individual attaches a subjective meaning to his behaviour – be it overt or covert, omission or acquiescence. Action is 'social' insofar as its subjective meaning takes account of the behaviour of others, and is thereby oriented in its course.[13]

Finally, Schutz invites us to re-examine the original constitution of the life-world which human beings take for granted in their 'natural attitude', through such devices as an assumed 'reciprocity of perspectives' and an 'interchangeability of standpoints', and which the social analyst rarely topicalizes, but which is an active site of culture regarded as a social process emergent from intentional social action. Schutz's theoretical initiatives are taken forward and developed in the work of Thomas Luckmann and Peter Berger which addresses the social construction of all cultural realities.

TALCOTT PARSONS AND THE GENERAL THEORY OF ACTION

Parsons, whose theory of the social system we considered earlier in relation to the concept of social structure, was attempting to provide a unifying scheme for the social sciences through a theory of action. He was also, however, concerned with a clarification of the concept of culture as the very context of social interaction.

> Perhaps the point may first be discussed briefly in relation to the problem of culture. In anthropological theory there is not what could be called close agreement on the definition of the concept of culture. But for present purposes three prominent keynotes of the discussion may be picked out: first, that culture is *transmitted*, it constitutes a heritage or a social tradition; secondly, that it is *learned*, it is not a manifestation, in particular content, of man's genetic constitution; and third, that it is *shared*. Culture, that is, is on the one hand the product of, on the other hand a determinant of, systems of human social interaction.[14]

Weber's ideas were clearly formative for Parsons, although the theoretical end product is less identifiable with its origins, than in the case of Schutz. Parsons was educated at Heidelberg and despite having just missed Weber's teaching he was much influenced by the neo-Kantian tradition and its insistence on establishing immutable categories as a basis for social and cultural understanding.

The beginning of theorizing for Parsons is twofold, being located in the problem of order, which led him to systems, and in the problem of control, which led him to the idea of social action. It is no simple matter to pin down an explicit definition of action in Parsons, but Rocher has attempted to distil one for us:

> Social action . . . is all human behaviour motivated and directed by the meanings which the actor discerns in the external world, meanings of which he takes account and to which he responds. So the essential feature of social action is the actor's sensitivity to the meanings of the people and things about him, his perception of these meanings and his reactions to the messages they convey.[15]

This resonates with Weber's definition but in Parsons's hands the concept transforms into an extreme level of abstraction. Within Parsons's theory of action the fundamental social object is the 'unit act' which, in combination with at least one other social object, comprises the 'action set' or 'interaction' between *ego* and *alter*. Interaction inhabits the cultural field which is made up of cultural, or what he sometimes calls symbolic, objects. Social action is utterly dependent upon its location within culture; it is (as shown in the above quote) essentially meaningful and therefore conducted through symbolism. Only by way of signs and symbols can the actor relate to his world; through symbolism he can assess, make judgements within and attempt to exercise some control over his environment. Without the cultural, the symbolic, for Parsons, there would be no interaction. It is both the medium of relation and the glue which cements people together in communication. If human action is always and everywhere supposed to exhibit the properties of a system then such systems are, in effect, intrinsically cultural, they are potentially infinite symbolic universes within which all conduct acquires meaning and is ascribed meaning by both *ego* and *alter*.

> Cultural objects are symbolic elements of the cultural tradition, ideas or beliefs, expressive symbols or value patterns so far as they are treated as situational objects by ego and are not 'internalized' as constitutive elements of the structure of his personality.[16]

As Parsons's reasoning unfolds we begin to recognize a continuity in meaning that sustains at all levels within the social system from the individual unconscious, the individual consciousness, the collective consciousness and even the system's functional prerequisites. This stable, unitary isomorphism ensures that the age-old sociological problem of order is held in check by the consensual complementarity of perspectives throughout the institutions of society and its culture.

> The most fundamental theorem of the theory of action seems to be that the *structure* of systems of action *consist* in institutionalized (in social and cultural systems) and/ or internalized (in personalities and organisms) patterns of cultural meaning. That this is not a proposition obvious to common sense is attested by the long and complex

history of behaviouristic and other reductionist theories of human behaviour. . . . [17]

What Parsons here refers to as a 'theorem' accounts for the reciprocity of the collective and individual perspectives by demonstrating that they are both grounded in culture patterns which are, in turn, realities within individual consciousness and the collective world of symbolism.

Parsons's obvious reification of the system set a problem of the demystification of action for his student Garfinkel who, applying inspirations from Schutz, set out to invert the Parsonian project and investigate 'the awesome mystery within', the daily affirmation of cultural reality through the mundane taken-for-granted practices of social action.

GEERTZ AND INTERPRETIVE ANTHROPOLOGY

Clifford Geertz is a contemporary American anthropologist who directly identifies himself with the *Verstende* tradition in the social sciences and locates the idea of culture firmly within the context of on-going, interpretive social action on the parts of both social actor and social theorist. He quite clearly understands culture as a symbolic network which, paradoxically for my classificatory scheme, he refers to as the 'semiotic' in the following quote.

> The concept of culture I espouse . . . is essentially a semiotic one. Believing, with Max Weber, that man is an animal suspended in webs of significance he himself has spun, I take culture to be those webs, and the analysis of it to be therefore not an experimental science in search of law but an interpretive one in search of meaning. It is explication I am after, construing social expressions on their surface enigmatical.[18]

Geertz, through his concern with active mental process, has much in common with the canons of classical idealism, though he attempts to render such distinctions defunct. His ethnographic practice which is his work, rather than his speculation, is very much embedded in the lived contexts of human societies as opposed to what he sees as a dominant modern intellectual attitude: 'anthropologists have shied away from cultural particularities when it came to a question of defining man and have taken refuge instead in bloodless universals'.[19] His symbolic, mentalist approach, relies very much on the description of what he sees as the layers of mediation, like mood, motivation and conception; between the systems of symbols and the facticities of everyday life. In this way he ranges through accounts of all aspects of culture from kinship, religion and politics to economics, addressing the social action of mind, both in the form of the conscious and the unconscious. This last phenomenon, the unconscious, puts him in a relation with psychoanalysis and structuralism, but again he marks out his difference, which is in terms of method. Geertz recommends the study of cultural phenomena through an engaged empirical fieldwork, an ethnography which is not a series of techniques but a relationship, an attitude. He seeks 'the enlargement of the universe of human discourse'[20] through an understanding of the meaning of a symbol or cluster of symbols for the people who are using them (what we used to call 'emic' as opposed to 'etic' analysis), a practical sense of location. This all stems from his important belief that culture is not a source of causality but a context of intelligibility. Geertz calls his method 'Thick Description', which goes beyond a description of 'what occurred' to the infinitely incompletable task of explaining the structures of signification within which 'what occurred' meaningfully took place.

The enthusiasm and optimism with which he puts forward his programme is quite compelling; and very much at odds with reductionist or essentialist accounts of culture.

> Cultural analysis is intrinsically incomplete. And, worse than that, the more deeply it goes the less complete it is. It is a strange science whose most telling assertions are its most tremulously based, in which to get somewhere with the matter at hand is to intensify the suspicion, both your own and that of others, that you are not quite getting it right. But that, along with plaguing subtle people with obtuse questions, is what being an ethnographer is like.[21]

LÉVI-STRAUSS AND STRUCTURALISM

This might be regarded as only a marginally appropriate location for a discussion of structuralism, but then so, perhaps, would any other placement within my classificatory scheme. Structuralism does not escape my categories, such as to justify a chapter of its

own, and it is considered later as a theory of cultural reproduction, so I will attempt to contain it here on the grounds of its
clear continuity with the tradition of philosophical idealism, the
backdrop to all the approaches to culture and social action treated
above. Lévi-Strauss did not assimilate his neo-Kantian concerns
within the context of the German academy but instead through
the auspices of the two French scholars whom he cites as formative in his thinking, namely, Durkheim and Mauss. Durkheim's
'social Kantianism' or 'soft idealism' we previously addressed in
relation to the symbolic versus the semiotic views of culture
and social structure. His collaborator and heir, Marcel Mauss,
advanced the idealist elements in accounting for social action
through his sense of 'collective representations'; these were more
generalized and reciprocal psychological dispositions common to
all humankind. He provided working examples of these two-way
senses of obligation and vocabularies of motivation through his
study of *The Gift*.

The universality of human cognitive action is central to Lévi-
Strauss's thought. Whatever the incessant variability of the forms
of human culture both across space (the 'synchronic') and through
time (the 'diachronic') it is asserted that the human mind has
always worked in the same way. Social action in the formation,
reproduction and even adaptation of actual cultures is, for the
purposes of structuralist analysis, a surface manifestation of a
series of deeply internalized master patterns at the deep structural
level of cognition. Particular cultures, then, are socio-historically
specific transformations of an unconscious, universal and immanent rule-system. The determinism is diffused through the specificity of the transformations.

Whether we are looking at Lévi-Strauss's analysis of kinship
systems through the exercise of the incest taboos that regulate
the exchange of women, Chomsky's account of 'linguistic universals' in direct relation to the infinite flexibility of any child's
capacity to acquire any language, or Piaget's investigations of the
genetic epistemology that ensures the commonality and regularity
of 'the child's' stages of cognitive development, we are in fact
looking past the transitory representations that make up modern
culture back to Descartes's positioning of 'man' at the hub of the
universe and then returning through Kant's location of that 'hub'
within the a priori continua of space, time and inevitably *causality*.

Structuralism enables us further to address the 'homologies', or similarities in configuration, between otherwise discrete cultural phenomena. We detect a seamless continuity between Roland Barthes contemplating the cultural significance of a meal in relation to the *choice* and *chain* provided through a menu, Jacques Lacan unscrambling the mis-transformations of schizophrenic *parole* in the face of the collective meanings of *la langue*, and Lévi-Strauss taking us through the unique production of a piece of orchestral music as the scored combination of *melody* and *harmony*.

Structuralism is, on reflection, a grand representation of the relation between culture and social action.

NOTES

[1] M. Weber, *The Methodology of the Social Sciences*, New York: Free Press (1949).

[2] T. Burger, *Max Weber's Theory of Concept Formation*, Durham, NC: Duke University Press (1976).

[3] H. Rickert, *Limits of the Concept Formation of the Natural Sciences* (trans. and ed. G. Oaks), Cambridge: Cambridge University Press (1986).

[4] T. Kuhn, *The Structure of Scientific Revolutions*, Chicago: Chicago University Press (1970).

[5] M. Weber, op. cit.

[6] T. Parsons, *The Structure of Social Action*, New York: Free Press (1951).

[7] M. Weber, *The Protestant Ethic and the Spirit of Capitalism*, New York: Free Press (1965).

[8] I. Zeitlin, *Ideology and the Development of Sociological Theory*, Englewood Cliffs, NJ: Prentice-Hall (1968); J. Lewis, *Max Weber and Value-Free Sociology*, London: Lawrence and Wishart (1975); P. Hirst, *Social Evolution and Sociological Categories*, London: Allen and Unwin (1976).

[9] D. Walsh, *Weber – Protestantism, Capitalism and Rationality: Culture and Structure in Western Civilization*, unpublished paper (1992).

[10] M. Weber, *The Protestant Ethic*, op. cit.

[11] D. Frisby and D. Sayer, *Society*, London: Tavistock (1986).

[12] A. Schutz, *Collected Papers* Vol. 1, The Hague: Martinus Nijhoff (1971), pp. 346–7.

[13] M. Weber, *Economy and Society*, New York: Free Press (1968).

[14] T. Parsons, *The Social System*, London: Routledge & Kegan Paul (1951), p. 15.

[15] G. Rocher, *Talcott Parsons and American Sociology*, London: Thomas Nelson (1974), pp. 28–9.

[16] T. Parsons, *The Social System*, London: Routledge & Kegan Paul (1951), p. 4.

[17] T. Parsons, 'The point of view of the author', in M. Black (ed.), *The Social Theories of Talcott Parsons*, Englewood Cliffs, NJ: Prentice-Hall (1961), p. 342.

[18] C. Geertz, *The Interpretation of Cultures*, London: Hutchinson (1975), p. 5.

[19] Ibid., p. 43.

[20] Ibid., p. 14.

[21] Ibid., p. 29.

4

Culture and materialism

In the case of art it is well known that certain flourishing periods are not by any means proportionate to the general development of society, hence to its material foundation, the skeleton, as it were, of its organization. For example the Greeks as compared with the moderns, or Shakespeare, in the case of certain art forms, e.g. the epos, it is even recognised that they can never be produced in their universal epoch-making classical form once artistic production as such has begun; hence that within the artistic world certain important formations are possible only at a primitive stage of art's development. If this applies to the interrelation between the various modes within the sphere of art, it is even less surprising that it should be the case in the relationship of the entire artistic realm to the general development of society.[1]

The work of Karl Marx, perhaps more than the writings of any other social theorist, illustrates the tropes and paradoxes of theorizing. Even though it might be argued that Marx's thought is challenged only by that of Jesus Christ and Sigmund Freud for the status of being the leading influence upon people's lives within the modern world, his is not a solitary message. It is certainly the case that there are far more Marxes available to us, through interpretation, than the one voice that we meet on the page. There are early and late Marx, humanist and scientific Marx, materialist and idealist Marx, structuralist, crude, Leninist Marx and so on. My point, in the context of a monograph on culture, is not to attempt to arrest this proliferation of versions, nor to point to the 'true' reading of Marx. Rather I hope to demonstrate that although I shall, in this chapter, cite Marx as the prime source of thinking about culture in relation to materialism, this too is only one formulation (albeit a predominant one) and his work may equally well be seen as contributing to the debate over culture and social action, stratification or social structure.

I will proceed to an analysis of various neo-Marxisms, from Gramsci and Lukács, to Goldmann and Benjamin, and of course to the work of Raymond Williams, and assess their varied contributions to our understanding of culture. Some of these are theories directly related to the material base, while others, following the influence of Hegel and phenomenology, move far more towards a semi-autonomous view of culture; to the point, almost, of excluding them from this category. Nevertheless, I shall justify this grouping on the grounds of each of the theorists contained here, demonstrating a primary allegiance to Marx in their thinking.

Let us begin by viewing Marx as the origin of this tradition of relating to cultural phenomena. Initially I want to view his work in relation to the classical epistemological dichotomy between idealism and materialism which, in the context of philosophy and social theory, has provided for the problem of knowledge being typically addressed through either a theory of *practical* reason, or through a theory of *pure* reason. The former, a theory of *practical* reason, stresses that humankind lives within a preconstituted, real world, which has an intrinsic, factual 'truth' status. Such a world impinges on the individual. The activity of 'knowing' is, then, the receiving of information from an external world. Humankind lives in a subservient relation with both culture and nature. We seek knowledge through the passive contemplation of objective structures. Such a deterministic theory is a variety of *materialism*.

A theory of *pure* reason, on the other hand, is premised on the centrality of humankind as a form of consciousness. That is to say that such a theory is concerned with the self-legislating capacity of the individual imposing itself upon the world. The act of 'knowing' transforms from a passive 'taking' or receiving process, to an active 'making' or constituting process. Such an unrestrained view of the mind would clearly instance a version of *idealism*.

In the former theory matter precedes mind and in the latter, mind precedes matter. Matter in each case may be understood as the deposition of representations that we would regard as the 'cultural'.

Let us pursue Marx's method towards an understanding of culture. One of Marx's conventionally characterized virtues is that he synthesized the dichotomy between materialism and idealism. His complexity derives from his inability to stabilize such a synthesis and from the compounding of his antecedent influences. His work was informed by the rationalist-idealism of Hegel, in terms of his sense of the 'pure consciousness'; and also by the materialism of Feuerbach (among others), in terms of his ideas of 'nature' and the 'material base'. This complexity is further compounded by his then having criticized, if not rejected, both such philosophies explicitly. This is not meant to imply that Marx was a mere compilation of influences or theoretical antecedents – his significance, and lasting contribution, derive from his innovation as a theorist as typified in the method that we now refer to as 'historical materialism'. Marx's corpus is widely referred to as materialistic, which is in part its intent and in part a legacy of Engels's subsequent mechanistic interpretation of his writings. Whereas Marx formulated the dialectic as a way of addressing *a* world, Engels, particularly in the *Dialectics of Nature*, produces it as a blueprint method for analysing *the* world. The concept of Nature for Engels, as for Feuerbach and the British empiricists, was conceptualized as inanimate, compelling and opaque matter. It was the form that preceded mind or consciousness; thus mind was seen as the product of matter. For Hegel, on the other hand, Nature was constructed as the 'Spirit' in a state of self-estrangement. Reason and ideas were rooted in humankind and there was no necessary external existence, that is, nothing was eventually alien to human consciousness and being. Hegel saw the idealist/materialist dichotomy as reflecting the master/slave patterning of relationships to the world – the former involved the imposition of ideas and the latter implied a structure imposing limits. Such a split in the possibilities of human consciousness between 'subject' and 'object' provided Marx with the grounds for his concept of 'alienation'. Marx's work, when viewed as inverting Hegel's thesis, can be read as having a primary concern with an engaged consciousness and the ultimate creative possibility of human self-emancipation or authenticity. Marx produces this through his concept of 'sensuousness'. He considered that Nature cannot be discussed as if it were separate from human action. This is because Nature, as a potential object for human cognition, has already been effected by previous human contact, and must continue to be provided for, or apprehended, by further human action in the form of theorizing. Thus Marx tends to speak of 'humanized nature' or 'sensuousness' rather than of objective factual data. It is as if all 'nature' pulsates with the productive endeavour of humanity.

> The chief defect of all hitherto existing materialism (that of Feuerbach included) is that the thing, reality, sensuousness, is conceived only in the form of the *object or of contemplation*, but not as *sensuous human activity*, *practice*, not subjectively. Hence, in contradistinction to materialism, the *active* side was developed abstractly by idealism – which, of course, does not know real, sensuous activity as such. Feuerbach wants sensuous objects, really distinct from the thought objects, but he does not conceive human activity itself as *objective* activity.[2]

Marx's analyses operate with the notion of reality as *Wirklichkeit*, i.e. as implying the initial creation of the world by human labour, and its continued production or shaping by the same means. In relation to this he directs us to the essentially conservative nature of both the classical doctrines of materialism and idealism – of Feuerbach's materialism he notes, in *The German Ideology*, that if the world is not the product of human thought and labour then how can we begin to change it; and of Hegel's speculative idealism Marx shows us that as such theorizing is utterly unreflexive about the grounds of its own production then, implicitly at least, it must accept those grounds as givens: 'It had not occurred to any one of these philosophers [the Hegelians] to inquire into the connection of German philosophy with German reality, the relation of their criticism to their own material surroundings.'[3]

Avineri[4] tells us that Marx saw that the constructive feature of human consciousness cannot be limited to mere cognition. Cognitive action must be seen as the whole process of the development and evolution of reality; the practice of getting acquainted with reality reflexively involves the action of shaping, formulating and changing reality. This is Marx's notion of 'praxis' and is instructive in understanding a Marxist approach to culture.

A strain or persistent problematic within Marx derives from his desire to envisage the conditions providing for the spontaneous and creative generation of praxis by people 'for themselves'. What, then, are the origins of praxis: what gives it birth? Having generated, in his own work, a method that, as it were, straddled or rather transcended the restrictions of the classical epistemological dichotomy between idealism and materialism, Marx was at pains to indicate the constraints that the bourgeois consciousness, and its positivistic knowledge, place upon the attainment of a life of praxis for all people. Consequently his dual concern with a description of consciousness and with a vision of a future 'possible' society lead him to theorize about imperfect modes of consciousness in terms of the concept of *ideology*. This, as we know, has become a pre-eminent concept in the understanding of culture and the analysis of cultural representations. It will be useful, at this point, to look at Marx's thesis contained in *The German Ideology*, as it is fundamental to what we now regard as a materialist view of the causal relation between any set of concrete states of affairs and the ideational, symbolic, or cultural manifestations that accompany them, or indeed, provide for them. In this major work Marx fulfils a twofold intention: at one level he dissociates himself from the system of Hegelian speculative philosophy that pervaded his day, and at another level he provides his original view of history. The former of these levels acts as a practical demonstration of the latter; that is to say that he instances the connection between his contemporary German philosophers and the particular social structure from which they emerged as a demonstration of 'the German ideology'. This ideology involves a distortion of the philosophers' views about their world because of their relationship to the sources of power and property in that world.

The German Ideology is a dynamic and poetic work which contemporary structuralist Marxists, following Althusser, have described as polemical, humanistic and itself ideological – indeed, a work to be dismissed as preceding the 'epistemological break' that generated the true scientific Marxism. However, the richness and inspiration of the text lies in its proliferation of formulations of the relationship between ideas and the material life. This is nowhere better demonstrated than in the classic quote, vivid in its metaphoricity:

The production of ideas, of conceptions, of consciousness, is at first directly interwoven with the material
activity and the material intercourse of men, the language
of real life. Conceiving, thinking, the mental intercourse
of men, appear at this stage as the direct efflux of their
material behaviour. The same applies to mental production as expressed in the language of politics, laws,
morality, religion, metaphysics etc. of a people. Men are
the producers of their conceptions, ideas, etc. – real,
active men, as they are conditioned by a definite development of their productive forces and of the intercourse
corresponding to these, up to its furthest forms. Consciousness can never be anything else than conscious
existence, and the existence of men is their actual life-
process. If in all ideology men and their circumstances
appear upside-down as in a *camera obscura*, this phenomenon arises just as much from their historical life-process
as the inversion of objects on the retina does from their
physical life-process.

In direct contrast to German philosophy which
descends from heaven to earth, here we ascend from
earth to heaven. That is to say, we do not set out from
what men say, imagine, conceive, nor from men as nar-
rated, thought of, imagined, conceived, in order to arrive
at men in the flesh. We set out from real, active men,
and on the basis of their real life-process we demonstrate
the development of the ideological reflexes and echoes
of this life-process. The phantoms formed in the human
brain are also, necessarily, sublimates of their material
life-process, which is empirically verifiable and bound to
material premises. Morality, religion, metaphysics, all the
rest of ideology and their corresponding forms of consciousness, thus no longer retain a semblance of indepen-
dence. They have no history, no development; but men,
developing their material production and their mental
intercourse, alter, along with this their real existence,
their thinking and the products of their thinking. Life is
not determined by consciousness, but consciousness by
life.[5]

Although the images and allusions within the passage provide, in
some senses, an unstable or inconsistent account of the relation

between the base and the superstructure, they point, overall, to a greater weight being given to the significance and efficacy of the material factors as the primary realities and the ideas and belief systems as being both secondary, and emergent from them. This reading of a materialist reduction is further supported by Marx's later discussion of the historical stages of social development, in terms of the different 'forms of production' like 'primitive communism', 'feudalism' and 'capitalism' itself. The modes of thought in each of these epochs emerges out of the relations that are established between people according to the economic division of labour. The way of life, or culture, of a people is, then, determined by economic forces; but, of course, it is more subtle than this. A culture is organized in relation to sets of interests within society and dominant interests are the articulation of power. Power, in turn, is rarely manifested as naked physical force, but is mediated through the existing systems of stratification within society (in relation to class, gender, race, ability, age and so on) which are, in general, taken for granted by most of the people, most of the time. In relation to culture Marx is telling us about the connection of ideas with the predominant system of stratification.

> The ideas of the ruling class are in every epoch the ruling ideas, i.e. the class which is the ruling *material* force of society, is at the same time its ruling *intellectual* force. The class which has the means of material production at its disposal, has control at the same time over the means of mental production, so that thereby, generally speaking, the ideas of those who lack the means of mental production are subject to it. The ruling ideas are nothing more than the ideal expression of the dominant material relationships, the dominant material relationships grasped as ideas; hence of the relationships which make the one class the ruling one, therefore, the ideas of its dominance. The individuals composing the ruling class possess among other things consciousness, and therefore think. Insofar, therefore, as they rule as a class and determine the extent and compass of an epoch, it is self-evident that they do this in its whole range, hence among other things rule also as thinkers, as producers of ideas, and regulate the production and distribution of the ideas

of their age: thus their ideas are the ruling ideas of the epoch.[6]

Through the concept of ideology which, as we shall see, has taken on many modern forms in pursuit of a theory of culture, Marx talks of the ideas of the ruling classes as legitimating and disguising their domination. Ideologies can be regarded as forceful explanatory devices which served, and continue to serve, a number of functions within the tradition of culture and materialism. Ideologies were, for Marx, phenomena in their own right; that is to say that as they were made up of sets of beliefs about the world, which nevertheless produced a distorted account of that world, it was essential that they be understood. This he achieved by relating their distortions to material reality, 'from heaven to earth', he contrasted 'appearances' with 'essences', for example, the relation of ideologists to the ownership of the means of production.

For Marx, ideologies began from a partial view of the world and were, significantly, unconscious of those beginnings. Indeed, their persuasiveness resided in the fact that they remained unaware of their own presuppositions. This, of course, is a feature of ideology that has altered dramatically in the context of a modern, commercial, technological culture that is largely organized through mass communication. Modern ideologists, like propagandists and advertisers, are only too conscious of the distortions that they artfully seek to propound, and modern theory has had to keep up with them through concepts like 'hegemony'. In Marx's view ideology mediated and refracted reality through a network of existing categories that were selected by the dominant group and acceptable to them, and we can witness here the manner in which political rhetoric, medical care, economic policy and educational knowledge is all conducted in terms of the discourse of the 'experts'. Successful ideological categories do not simply enable the purposes of an elite, or a select group within a culture; more significantly they disempower the majority through mystification, ignorance or feelings of inadequacy. Ideologies, then, generalize special and limited interests; they make the interests of some appear congruent with the interests of all. When someone informs you that something is 'for your own good', this is usually the time for the ideological detector warnings to sound the alarm! Another critical feature of ideological knowledge, within the context of an analysis of culture, is its capacity to generate a practical sense of consensus – a particularly important function in the context of a dispute over whether culture is the whole way of life of a people, or just the symbolic heritage of excellence in the appreciative possession of a select group, or if, indeed, whether a quasi-compatibility can be achieved between the two. Ideologies strive for consensus in as much as they play a significant part in maintaining order without force, by securing the assent of the oppressed, the exploited, the underclass, the needy and those dispossessed of cultural capital. This they achieve through a sophisticated and multi-layered network of iconography. They proliferate with images. Images of the dominant classes for themselves, as 'preservers of standards', 'guardians of the cultural heritage', 'upholders of reason, or civilization' etc . . . images of the dominant classes for other groups, as 'those who know best', 'those with our best interest at heart', 'those committed to the good of all' etc . . . images of other classes as perhaps 'less able' and 'in need of leadership', and . . . images of those classes for themselves: 'I may not know much about art, but I know what I like.' This iconography is not simply constituted through a series of labels that people take off when they go to school, apply for jobs, attend art galleries or exercise their vote. These images become a cognitive style, they become part of the way that people interpret their own conditions, and thus such images restrict people's scope for conceiving of alternatives. The culture that liberates the few through the enlightenment of their higher education, or through their life 'as a journey to Mozart', becomes simultaneously the prison and the exclusion of the many. Having said this it should not be forgotten that Marx, Engels, Lenin and Trotsky all had fairly 'high-art' tastes and were more in favour of 'raising up' mass standards than of destroying high culture. Marx also talks of 'all' classes having ideas, some, perhaps, having revolutionary ideas; and that all class ideas, as ideologies, strive to present particular interests as being identical with the interests of all. In this instance, by providing ideas as weapons within the class struggle, Marx may now be heard as saying that ideas, and not just the material base, have a causal efficacy. The central point, however, is the acknowledgement of the force of dominant thought systems and their relation to material conditions in any historical period. Classes are, of course, real, but at another level they may be viewed as metaphors for particular language games and forms of discourse within a culture. A bourgeois culture is an instance of the form of consciousness within a community that conceptualizes human-kind, and its knowledge, as ordered by objectivities, or material structures that are other than and in excess of itself. Such a community might know the price of everything and the value of nothing, it would view knowledge as a possession, treat art as property and regard the artistic enterprise in terms of profit and loss. Its discourse, and the metaphors of its culture, would be those of the market place. Seen in this way, the communist utopia is never simply reducible to a concrete structural state of affairs located in a future time, it speaks rather of a reflexive community of people wedded to practical reason, authentically realizing themselves as theorists, that is, as constructors of worlds.

Although sociology has largely treated such ideas as ideology, class domination and economic determinism as concrete descriptions of real states of affairs, in the manner of positivism, what is, in part, being recommended here is that such notions may be treated as Marx's analytic rules for assembling worlds. So, for example, the importance of 'ideology' in the understanding of culture can be seen as not the impersonal effects of the force of ideas upon the individual, but rather as Marx's formulation of a meaningful environment constructed in terms of a typical actor within materialism. Ideology thus assigns a rule of relevance to the conduct of actors.

Perhaps the next major development in the chronology of Marx's method, or 'Wissenschaft', is to be found in the Introduction to the Critique of Political Economy of 1857, leading to its 'scientific' fruition in Das Kapital. In the former work Marx distinguishes two sorts of concepts, those that are historically located and related to contemporary realities, and those that, through their abstraction, are universal and uncluttered by the particulars of any historical moment (like population). Traditional political economy begins its analysis with these abstractions and cannot therefore, Marx asserts, ever aspire to account for the real material conditions of an epoch. His method, in contradistinction, recommends a synthesis of the real and the historically located in order to arrive at a constructive, materialist unification of theory/practice; this he characterizes as 'the correct scientific method'. For Marx, the real world remains external to, and outside of the intellect so long as a purely theoretical attitude is adopted to it. Marxist analysis regards 'reality' as the precondition of understanding and also as the point of origin of both perception and imagination. Thus thought is an act of transformation, an act of production within which concepts are formed. For Marx the appropriate scientific concepts are the products of historical conditions; certain transformations are possible only under certain historical conditions. Concepts achieve their full validity only under the historical conditions of their occurrence; this we can see as a clear assault on the positivism of social theory that attempts to operate with context-free categories of analysis. This attack on positivism is crucial to Marx's epistemology and clearly underlies his criticism of classical political economy. He states: 'Economists explain how production takes place in the above mentioned relations, but what they do not explain is how these relations themselves are produced, that is, the historical moment that gave them birth'[7] and here he is demanding that the theorist should ground his or her own accounts of the world in real, material conditions. He concludes: 'Economic categories are only the theoretical expressions, the abstractions of the social relations of production'[8] and so also, we might add with an attention to this point in his method, are the categories of cultural analysis!

Finally we should look to *Das Kapital* as the completion of Marx's methodological project; what Althusser regards as the birth of the 'mature' and 'scientific' Marxism. This is a massive work containing sporadic references to methodology and the theory of ideology one of which, referring to 'Wages', I use later in an analysis of cultural reproduction. Here I shall address the section on 'Commodity Fetishism' which concerns the appearance/reality distinction. This distinction is central to a Marxist approach to cultural representations. Where the productive base of a society is concerned with making commodities for exchange in the market place, social relations form between the producers based on an assumed relation between the commodities (e.g. producer of high-value goods [head] having superior status to producer of low-value goods [hand]). These social relations, Marx tells us, take on a 'misleading appearance'. This appearance has to do with the imagery of the products, that is, the way that they present themselves to the producers. All commodities are assigned values in the market, all commodities are connected to one another according to those values, and the producers have a social relationship according to those values. However, these values, which we routinely take for granted as objective, are themselves bound to no perceptible property of the commodities. These appearance values pass themselves off as the social relations between commodities in the market place, but the 'real' value of a commodity can only be the expression of human labour spent in its production. The 'true' relation, disguised by the supposed relation between things, is the social relation between producers. The appearance is an ideological mystification of the real, essential relation. The Marxist analysis of culture always looks beyond to the hidden relation which preserves the status quo.

LUKÁCS: REALIST AESTHETICS AND THE TOTALITY

Let us move now to the input of the original corpus of Marx's materialist method to the contributions of certain neo-Marxists to our understandings of human culture.

> Any Marxist who is at all concerned with philosophical problems necessarily starts out from the anthropocentric view of history which Marx and Engels inherited from Kant and the German Enlightenment generally: man stands at the centre of the man-created world of society, and this 'world' includes the sphere of art which reflects a particular dimension of the human spirit.[9]

Thus Lichtheim introduces us to the aesthetics of Georg Lukács, the Hungarian philosopher, whose creative period of political and cultural analysis extended from the beginning of the century until the late 1960s.

Lukács has been described as 'the Marx of aesthetics', a soubriquet not wholly without grounds but one that in many senses maligns his life project. He cannot be pigeon-holed as merely a philosopher, in the sense of a speculative armchair theorist, and he cannot be read as disposing his intellect solely in the pursuit of artistic representations, a seemingly elitist activity. Lukács was a theorist of immense complexity; although Hungarian in origin and occupying much of his time actively involved in Hungarian politics and their academy, most of his education and maturation as a thinker took place in Germany where he encountered, and was greatly influenced by, German Romanticism in the form of Dilthey, Rickert, Simmel and Max Weber; many of the scholars, it will be noted, who appear under my category of 'Culture and Social Action'. It was here, through his own grounding in Hegel (a lifelong driving force) that he developed his critique and resistance to both neo-Kantian idealism, and also the irrationalism of Nietzsche; all of this was to form a backdrop to his later dismissals of bourgeois modernism for its individualism and decadence. What this period also produced for him was a primary, and typically European, commitment to metaphysics, a resistance to positivism and a sense of his theorizing as social and essentially political; all sources of his central concept of a 'totality'. He went on to work in Vienna at a time when Freud's theories were paramount, when the logical positivists were an active and influential group, and when Wittgenstein's first monumental treatise on linguistic philosophy was emerging; Lukács remained utterly untouched by any of these movements. These passionate allegiances, exclusions and contradictions figure strongly in his ideas. Concurrent with and, for him, utterly integrated with his intellectual development was his intense involvement in, and contribution to, the development of European socialist culture. He was a political activist playing a leading role in the unsuccessful Hungarian Revolution of 1919, a Communist Party member and, for a period, a Commissar. Such was his influence and the level of his recognition that his *History and Class Consciousness* caused disquiet at the highest levels of the Soviet hierarchy because of its Hegelian origins and its unholy amalgamation of Leninism with ideas derived from Rosa Luxemburg, and it was denounced as 'deviationist'; Lenin had occasion to rebuke him for his 'ultra-leftist' actions; and eventually under the vicious, suspicious and retributive regime of Stalin he was drawn, through fear for his life, to publicly modify and reformulate many of his views into a form that even his most ardent admirers have difficulty in reconstructing as anything other than slogan and propaganda. His concept of a 'totality', which he was to apply consistently to the analysis of the work of art, or indeed any cultural product, can be seen to be equally applicable to the style of his life. He believed in total philosophical systems, like Hegel's, which required an initial commitment to the nature of being; as opposed to the English replacement of metaphysics with a bland empiricism, supported by science and common sense. His anthropocentrism, referred to earlier, is an ontological belief in the primacy and purpose of human being, the constitution of culture through human action and the vivid possibilities presented for change through history. All of this in the context of a modern world, an impelling materiality which, though understood dialectically, nevertheless threatened to oppress the life-force of the '*Geist*' emerging through creativity;

this led directly to his views on 'alienation' and 'reification' as man-made, yet material constraints upon people freely expressing their unique intent. Lukács's belief in totalities, as philosophical systems, extended, without a break, to the necessity of the integration of thought and action; hence his persistent and vigorous political involvement, whatever its implications. Perhaps his fundamental motivation, as a systems philosopher, was to produce a theory of aesthetics that would achieve on behalf of the new culture of East European socialism what Hegel and German idealism had achieved for the modern western bourgeois world. He generated a tradition of socialist scholarship that was original, revolutionary and worthy of intellectual consideration. This is no slight achievement in an historical period penetrable only by the intelligentsia, and not known for the open policy of its corpus of knowledge. As Steiner put it, 'Lukács has always held himself responsible to history. This has enabled him to produce a body of critical and philosophical work intensely expressive of the cruel and serious spirit of the age'.[10] This is, perhaps, the positive legacy of Lukács's 'Devil Pact'.

For the Marxist Lukács (as opposed to the youthful neo-Kantian who authored *The Theory of the Novel*) the relation between politics, art and culture became inextricable. A philosopher's view of the world, like that of the creative artist, is interwoven with the class struggle. This, of course, directs us to the centrality of aesthetics and the singular obsession, and indeed axiom, in Lukács's ideas, that 'realism' in art and philosophy produces not just another version of the world, but it actually portrays the world (the actual concept that Lukács employs is to 'reflect' the world). This is no reversion to a positivistic correspondence theory of truth; it means, instead, that whatever reifications and distortions the social world may have passed through and whatever formal mediations art or philosophy may require, the outcome of a realist project is to enable humankind to perceive its own true nature. 'Realism is not one style among others; it is the basis of literature.'[11] This potentially constraining assertion provided the basis for his criticism of modernist, formalist and experimental art as deviating from a recognition of the truth of the human condition enmeshed in the totality of social, economic, political and historical conditions. The social relation becomes the basis of a theory of culture, and the form of any cultural representation must be dictated by its content, which is that very social relation: '. . .there is no content of which Man

himself is not the focal point'.[12] Modernist art, by deviating into
the bizarre and alienating circumstances of contemporary life,
descends into decadent subjectivism; alternatively such bourgeois
enterprise attempts literal description, an accurate representation
echoing the empiricism of its sciences; this is the descent into
naturalism. Such work, through its insistence on description as
opposed to narration, leaves humankind in stasis. Critical realist
art and literature, on the other hand, has to be dynamic; it
projects its characters into the historical process and provides
them with direction, development and the motivation and intention to create change. A dynamic literature, a socialist realism,
was, for Lukács, a mirror of the dominant movement of its time.
Realist art carries with it universal and integrated forms of beauty
and truth which are in opposition to the fragmentation and mystification that is created through a capitalist division of labour.

> The goal for all great art is to provide a picture of reality
> in which the contradiction between appearance and
> reality, the particular and the general, the immediate and
> the conceptual, etc., is so resolved that the two converge
> into a spontaneous integrity. . . . The Universal appears
> as the quality of the individual and the particular, reality
> becomes manifest and can be experienced within appear-
> ance.[13]

The totality of human life is systematically eroded through the
separation, alienation, isolation and consequent despair that is
engendered within capitalist social structures. This is the 'angst'
that modernist literature, such as Kafka's, and Expressionist art,
such as that of Munch, van Gogh and Kokoschka, seem to cele-
brate through an exaltation of the subjective, inner self.

> Art functions aesthetically to create an enriched self-
> consciousness. . . . The essence of all art [for Lukács]
> lies in its realist aesthetics, its grasp of social totality and
> the universal within social development. Art is thus the
> medium of the 'correct' education of humanity, a self-
> enclosed totality pointing the way towards utopia.[14]

GRAMSCI: CULTURAL HEGEMONY AND THE INTELLECTUALS

It would be hard to imagine two people more different than
Lukács: '. . . the one major philosophic talent to have emerged

from the grey servitude of the Marxist world'[15] and Antonio Gramsci, the Italian communist, whose writings have been seen to '. . . broaden, "democratize", and enrich Lenin's strategy of socialist revolution'.[16] Though separated by only six years at birth, the aristocratic East European inhabited a very different class position and enjoyed a different life experience from the small, sickly, physically deformed Sardinian. They are, it is clear, bound together by their impassioned commitment to the cause of social-ism, but also through the tasteless metaphor of 'imprisonment', Lukács in Stalinist dogma and Gramsci in the inhuman conditions of Mussolini's prisons, which claimed almost a quarter of his short life. Although Lukács opened up the possibility of a populist engagement in the cultural process through his notions of realism and the totality, it cannot be denied that his work persistently addressed what we have referred to as 'high culture', and rested on the primacy of great art and the leadership of the great artist as 'partisan for the truth'. Gramsci, on the other hand, through his original address of the role of the intellectual, the necessity of an active cultural politic, and the analysis of hegemony, with its necessary resistance through counter-hegemony, provides for a different kind of understanding and engagement with popular culture.

> The more the cultural life of an individual is broad and well-grounded, the closer his opinions are to the truth, they can be accepted by everyone: the more numerous the individuals of broad and well-grounded culture, the more popular opinions approach to truth – that is to say contain the truth in an immature and imperfect form which can be developed till it reaches maturity and per-fection. It follows from this that the truth must never be presented in a dogmatic and absolute form, as if it were mature and perfect. The truth, because it can spread, must be adapted to the historical and cultural conditions of the social group in which we want it to spread.[17]

These ideas, combined with elements and revisions from Althusser, have become very influential in the development of cultural studies and the sociology of culture in Britain, as we shall see later.

The scope of Gramsci's substantive interests is attested to by the magnitude of topics that are addressed in *The Prison Note-books*, ranging from education, philosophy, issues of gender,

history, the intelligentsia, and specifically culture itself. The overall motif, however, is the generation and elaboration of an original Marxist theory suitable for the analysis of the conditions of
an advanced capitalist culture. Gramsci's thought reveals an
active and volatile theorist who emphasizes the intentional
character of political action in opposition to those theories extol-
ling the inexorable and deterministic laws of capitalist development. The path to socialism is neither singular nor straight, and
requires a relocation of the individual in the vortex of revolutionary struggle. To this end, his own writing was always conceived
of as a revolutionary act, not an act of speculation or description,
but a dynamic in the process of change. This drive is to be
systematically fired by the cultural critic's internalization of the
notion of 'praxis', the conscious unification of theory and practice, logos and eros, thought and action, subject and object. Life
is project and project is polemic.

> The philosophy of praxis is a reform and a development
> of Hegelianism; it is a philosophy that has been liberated
> (or is attempting to liberate itself) from any unilateral or
> fanatical ideological elements; it is consciousness full of
> contradictions, in which the philosopher himself, under-
> stood both individually and as an entire group, not only
> grasps the contradictions, but posits himself as an
> element of the contradiction and elevates this element to
> a principle of knowledge and therefore of action.[18]

The most significant contribution of Gramsci's thinking to the
Marxist tradition, and also to the analysis of social and cultural
formations, has been through his original discussion of the nature
and functioning of ideology invoking his concept of 'hegemony'.
This concept, most particularly, updates the theory of ideology
into the context of late modernity. Whereas Hegel had divided
authority into the two spheres of 'political society' and 'civil
society', Gramsci reworked this distinction into the operation of
two modes of control, domination and consent. The former is
the hard and brutal edge of power, more typical of an older
order in society. Modern political structures function through the
allegiance and incorporation of the controlled. The implication
here is of a politic of voluntarism; the ideological strategy is, in
fact, one of coercion, persuasion and cooperation but the
coercion is 'soft', the persuasion 'hidden' and the cooperation
'one-sided'; what retains is the appearance and experience of

voluntarism. Hegemony is the principle that enables this tacit consent through popular 'consensus'. Hegemony mediates between the individual and the exercise of choice, and hegemony permeates the structures within which choices are made possible; it alters our knowledge about the world. 'The realization of an apparatus of hegemony, in so far as it creates a new ideological soil and determines a reform of consciousness and of the methods of knowledge, is a fact of knowledge, a philosophical fact.'[19]

All elements of the superstructure contrive to exert ideological hegemony within the culture, from religion, to education, the mass media, law, mass culture, sport and leisure and so on. Within an advanced mass society with mass education, mass literacy and mass media all operating through a high level of technology, the centre of power becomes far more adept and artful in reaching out to embrace the periphery.

> The 'normal' exercise of hegemony in the area which has become classical, that of the parliamentary regime, is characterized by the combination of force and consensus which vary in their balance with each other, without force exceeding consensus too much. Thus it tries to achieve that force should appear to be supported by the agreement of the majority, expressed by the so-called organs of public opinion – newspapers and associations. . . . Midway between consensus and force stands corruption or fraud (which is characteristic of certain situations in which the exercise of the function of hegemony is difficult, making the use of force too dangerous).[20]

Outside the institutional context, hegemonic power is rendered viable and permanent through cultural values, norms, beliefs, myths and traditions which appear to belong to the people and have a life outside particular governments and class systems; they nevertheless serve to perpetuate the going order. Modern politics administrates not so much through power as through authority, and authority requires acquiescence or 'legitimacy'. Because such a system invites, and depends upon consent, it rewards its populace with cultural stability; a fact of their own making.

> The fact of hegemony undoubtedly presupposes that the interests and tendencies of the groups over which hegemony is to be exercised are taken into account, that there is a certain equilibrium of compromise, that, that

is, the ruling group makes sacrifices of an economic-corporate kind, but it is also indubitable that such sacrifices and such compromises cannot effect what is essential.[21]

Gramsci's analysis of the role of intellectuals in the cultural process (an issue always critical to Marxist theory as intellectuals are either in the vanguard of reaction to social change or are the essential class traitors in the march to revolution), is both to democratize the role and then to incorporate its specialisms and vitality. The democratization takes place by dispossessing the group of the ownership and production of culture; to be intellectual is a universal function.

Each man, finally, outside of his professional activity, carries on some form of intellectual activity, that is, he is a 'philosopher', an artist, a man of taste, he participates in a particular conception of the world, has a conscious line of moral conduct, and therefore contributes to sustain a conception of the world or to modify it, that is, to bring into being new modes of thought.[22]

The sphere of intellectual activity within a society, therefore, does not belong to a cultural elite who practise a specialized cognitive style and a shared epistemology, but rather it manifests itself as an integral segment of political action that is rooted in the daily lives and culture of the people as a whole.

The mode of being of the new intellectual can no longer consist in eloquence, which is an exterior and momentary mover of feelings and passions, but in active participation in practical life, as constructor, organizer, 'permanent persuader', and not just simple orator.[23]

Gramsci then describes the two kinds of intellectual, the 'traditional' who upholds the old order (and bears a striking resemblance to the Catholic Church), and the 'organic' who emerges as representative of his time to articulate the new order. They are, respectively, part of the problem and part of the solution.

GOLDMANN: GENETIC STRUCTURALISM

. . . the dialectical aesthetic sees every work of art as the expression, in the specific language of literature, painting, music or sculpture etc. of a world vision; and that, as we would expect, this vision also expresses itself on numerous other philosophical and theological levels, as well as on that of men's everyday actions and activity. The essential criteria by which the aesthetic of dialectical materialism judges the value of any expression of a world vision are the inner coherence of the work of art and especially the coherence between form and content.[24]

Lucien Goldmann was a sociologist, humanist thinker and cultural critic, born in Romania just before the First World War. His writings on the production and the place of art within an analysis of culture provide a complex, and often challenging, contribution to the tradition of materialistic Marxism within which the author locates himself. Part of his originality derives from his consistent desire to generate a dialectical method for the analysis of literary 'creativity' (a term that he preferred to 'production' on the basis of his espousal of the place of subjectivity in the process). Throughout his work Goldmann remained as resistant to the crude reductionism of most conventional, mechanistic, materialist explanations of cultural representations and forms for its strictures, closures and oppressive triviality, as he was vehemently opposed to the reality and practice of Soviet communism. Indeed, his sustained lack of a party line and his deviationist adoration of the young Marx (of *The German Ideology*) and of Hegelianism, have led some to suggest that he may not be a Marxist at all; but this is merely an ideological critique, not a fact.

Goldmann developed an approach to the analysis of literary and artistic practice that he referred to as 'genetic structuralism'. This method found its roots in the '*Geist*' of German idealism, particularly in the form of Hegelian dialectics; the Marxist view that culture is the expression of a group consciousness directed towards changing institutionalized social and political structures; the concept of a 'totality' deriving from the early, 'pre-Soviet' Lukács; and finally from the powerful sense of immanent cognitive categories that he found in the developmental structuralism of Piaget with whom he worked for a number of years. Genetic structuralism begins with the premise that any analysis of intellectual creativity and its relationship with practical social existence is concerned with the cognitive categories that shape both realms of the imaginary and the real. Thus, Goldmann argues that the significant literature (or any important art) of any historical period constitutes a nascent articulation of the emerging 'world vision' of a new social order.

> What is a world vision? It is not an immediate, empirical fact, but a conceptual working hypothesis indispensable to an understanding of the way in which individuals actually express their ideas. Even on an empirical plane, its importance and reality can be seen as soon as we go beyond the ideas or work of a single writer, and begin to study them as part of a whole.[25]

Goldmann ties this in with the concept of social class:

> World vision is a convenient term for the whole complex of ideas, aspirations and feelings which links together the members of a social group . . . and which opposes them to members of other social groups. This is . . . a tendency which really exists among the members of a certain social group who all attain this class consciousness in a more or less coherent manner. . . . In a few cases . . . there are exceptional individuals who actually achieve or who come very near to achieving a completely integrated and coherent view of what they and the social class to which they belong are trying to do. The men who express this vision on an imaginative or conceptual plane are writers and philosophers, and the more closely their work expresses this vision in its complete and integrated form, the more important does it become. They then achieve the maximum possible awareness of the social group whose nature they are expressing.[26]

This new and emergent social order does not have to be a socialist order; it is here that he disagrees with Lukács over the singularity, necessity and grinding inevitability of the relationship between 'good art' and realism. Other artistic and literary forms befit change and different world visions; indeed, proletarian criticism alone cannot be trusted with the future of cultural creativity or with the forging of political utopias. Great art or literature is not, for Goldmann, locked into a predictable relation with the inevitable socialist entelechy, it extols the spirit of its time, the Hegelian '*Geist*'; this is what reading, criticism or appreciation seeks to reveal.

A second original and significant feature of Goldmann's

method is his relocation of subjectivity. In contrast with most other structuralisms we find no 'death of the author' here. The active or dynamic subject is saluted as the very centre of cultural creativity. This active subject, like the developing, immanent subject in Piaget, is proactive in the creation and transformation of representative cultural forms; but these forms, though real and tangible in their manifestations, derive from structures that are cognitive and collective, as are the subjectivities themselves. This means that in order to reconcile the notion of a totality, a holistic structure, with a creative constitutive individual, within the demands of a structuralist theory Goldmann creates the 'collective subject' or the 'transindividual subject'. A cognitive structure, that enables individual action, is the outcome of the combined conduct of groups of people who have lived through shared experiences and devised collective strategies through which to handle and control them. So cognitive structures, that make for active subjects, are like collective consciousnesses, they are social phenomena and not the province of individual psychologies.

The structural determinism now appears to overwhelm the voluntarism of the author; the author becomes a midwife, inducing the vision from the womb of the world. As Swingewood puts it: 'Goldmann's structuralism in effect suppresses the dialectic of subject and object, author and text, author and group transforming the living relations into a schematic formalism.'[27]

Goldmann's appraisal of the problematic of contemporary culture rests on an extension of Lukács's concept of reification, stemming from the original Marxian views on commodity fetishism. The world appears, through the advance of capitalism and its permeation into civil society, to have dispensed with a real grasp of use value under the consuming onslaught of exchange value. Goldmann charts this development in the novel alongside the changes in the modes of production in society. This enables the diachronicity of his structuralism to exist alongside the synchronicity of his analysis of cognitive forms.

Whatever its shortcomings in ingesting aspects of its own idealism, Goldmann's work goes a considerable distance towards achieving a semi-autonomous view of culture within the context of a Marxist materialism.

> In principle, religion, morality, art and literature are neither autonomous and independent of economic life, nor simply reflections of it. However, in a capitalist

society they tend to become so, as the economic system of that society progressively controls all aspects of it.[28]

BENJAMIN: MODERNITY, CULTURAL PRODUCTION AND THE AURA

Walter Benjamin, the German cultural critic, born before the turn of the century and dying by his own hand to avoid Nazi persecution during the Second World War, produced a broad spectrum of writings around the issues of aesthetics, the production and reception of cultural forms and artefacts, technicization, literary criticism and urban life; all within a materialist framework. Although a difficult thinker to categorize, he falls well within the definition of a theorist of modernity. Indeed, along with Nietzsche, whose doctrine of 'the eternal return' he shared, he has been described as producing an archaeology and explanation of the pre-history of modernity.

> . . . no epoch has existed that did not feel itself, in the most eccentric sense, to be 'modern' and consider itself to be standing immediately before an abyss. The despairing, wide-awake consciousness, standing immersed in a decisive crisis, is chronic in humanity. Every period appears to itself as unavoidably new. This 'modernity', however, is precisely that which is diverse just like the diverse aspects of one and the same kaleidoscope.[29]

Benjamin, who regarded himself as very much a critical socialist, producing a sociology of art that has many continuities with the programme of Lukács's aesthetics and working in association with Korsch, and also Brecht; was clearly concerned with the political context of a culture, and of art's political impact on the culture of its time. One of his oft-quoted remarks is to the effect that '. . . while Fascism aestheticized politics, Communism politicized art'. Clearly there is a strong sense of the material integrity between politics and culture at work here. Despite the delicacy of his theorizing the compulsion of the materialist reduction is often felt in his work. Indeed, Adorno, a leading member of the Frankfurt Institute with which Benjamin had a continuing association, had occasion, during the 1930s, to be extremely critical of Benjamin's analysis of the city, which was centred on Paris, for its crude reductionist materialism. In his two most significant essays on cultural production, *The Author as Producer* and *The Work of Art in the Age of Mechanical Reproduction* Benjamin develops his thesis concerning the central irony of 'newness' and the creative project within modernity. While the Frankfurt School were introducing their ideas of the rise of the 'culture industry' and of 'mass culture' (which we shall consider in the next chapter), and regarding these historical developments with no small sense of unease, given their grounding in the '*Kultur*' of German Romanticism, Benjamin was formulating a view of the same processes with a double-edged optimism. The modern age, among other things, produces its identity and reproduces the signs of that identity through the mechanics of technology. It has accelerated change through the development of its technologies of production – the very origins and necessary material grounds of postmodernity's supposed simulacra. The 'good' in these developments, as Benjamin saw it, was the inevitable assault on bourgeois, elite culture. In a time before the possibility of mechanical production, or more significantly, mass reproduction, the purity, singularity, spontaneity and creativity of the art object – be it a Mahler symphony or a painting by Manet – belonged in the privileged possession of that section of the population, clearly marked out by their class position, who had access to its consumption.

This, Benjamin tells us, is the 'aura' of a work of art. Viewed in this way mechanical reproduction has an emancipatory potential, whether in the form of videos, long-playing records, musak, Athena reproductions or even imitation jewellery; all people, it is alleged, can have access to art. The 'bad' in these developments is, simultaneously and ironically, recognized by Benjamin in the commodification of culture itself. The de-aurification of the art work is a loss; in bringing the art object closer to more people, the democratization of cultural production, it is brought nearer only as a commodity and the essence of its creation is lost, which is what we see in Picasso T-shirts, or Pavarotti as a football anthem.

> Benjamin defines the aura as 'the unique phenomenon of a distance, however close [an object] may be'. The aura testifies to the *authority* of art in its cultic form, its condition of inimitable uniqueness, a singularity in time and space which is the hallmark of its authenticity. 'The uniqueness of a work of art is inseverable from its being embedded in the fabric of tradition.'[30]

Art, for Benjamin, as an expression in a culture, is no part of a world view, as Goldmann sees it, nor even the totality of Lukács, it is a fragment, a microcosm.

> Love for the object holds on to the radical uniqueness of the work of art and takes as its starting point the creative point of indifference where insight into the nature of the 'beautiful' or 'art' is confined to and permeates the totally unique and individual work. It enters into its inner nature as into that of a monad, which . . . has no window, but which embodies in itself the miniature of the whole.[31]

Art has a material basis in the structure and organization of a society, in its beliefs, its means of production and its political arrangements. To this extent Benjamin's ideas are in line with the predominant view within modernism, that art is intimately linked with the grounds of its production. If non-democratic art rests on monopolistic auras, for example, the private languages of story-telling that typify the specialisms and expertise of bourgeois communities, then socialist art must be based on collective, shared, egalitarian forces in modern society; the facts of realism. Capitalism, and its accompanying industrialism have altered the space between its production and its reception. 'To perceive the aura of an object we look at means to invest it with the ability to look at us in return . . . in a concept of aura . . . comprises the "unique manifestation of difference" '[32] Benjamin is demonstrating to us that each mode of cultural production carries with it, in a relatively fixed relation, a specific mode of reception. In his work on Baudelaire and through his engagement with the Parisian Arcades project, Benjamin developed a series of metaphors apposite to the appreciation of cultural representations through modernity, for example the crowd, the labyrinth and, perhaps most poignantly, the *flâneur*, the trifler, the wanderer of the boulevards. Each of these senses of the 'receptive' life of the modern person linked consciousness and art and social structure in a tight, irredeemable complex, an aesthetic complex so reductively materialistic, in fact, that Adorno renounced it as lacking dialectics and mediation. The whole social process, that is culture, seems to be subsumed by the state of the material, and in this case mechanical, world for Benjamin. The shortcomings of an otherwise insightful body of theorizing are well summarized by Swingewood when he says:

A theory of production clearly requires a theory of society, but Benjamin failed to theorise the specific underlying structural trends of advanced capitalism: on the one hand the capitalist social formation becomes increasingly centralised (primarily in the economic and political sphere) and collectivist (trade unions, political parties) while on the other evolving a complex multiplicity of autonomous institutions located within civil society. Benjamin held a simplified Marxist concept of capitalist economy and culture as closed structures with technology constituting the means of democratising and politicising art: no longer based on ritual, art flows from another practice, that of politics.[33]

RAYMOND WILLIAMS: A LONG REVOLUTION

The contribution made by Raymond Williams to our contemporary work in cultural studies and the sociology of culture is immense. His writings in the area are legion with, perhaps, *Culture and Society*, *The Long Revolution*, *Keywords* and *Culture* providing the obvious landmarks in the evolution of his thesis. Following this chronology we can witness a shift in style from that of a left-wing professor of English into a more fully fledged materialist critique of contemporary culture based as much on an understanding of sociology and anthropology as on the English literary tradition. This is not to suggest that any of his works demonstrate less than a highly informed and articulate contribution to the culture of socialism in this country, or an insightful analysis of many forms of mass and popular culture. His project may be interpreted as truly counter-hegemonic, in Gramsci's sense. It began, alongside his commitment to workers' education and the celebration of the working-class culture of his youth, as an intellectual opposition to the reactionary seizure of 'culture' by the bourgeois tradition of Quiller-Couch, Leavis and Eliot. Williams was radically opposed to the ideology of elitism exercised in that very academic tradition that had enabled him to speak with authority.

There was a question for me whether I should write a critique of that ideology . . . or . . . to try to recover the true complexity of the tradition it had confiscated – so that the appropriation could be seen for what it was. . . .

> I settled for the second strategy. For it allowed me to
> refute the increasing contemporary use of the concept of
> culture against democracy, socialism, the working class
> or popular education, in terms of tradition itself.[34]

Williams formulated a tradition of discourse about the concept
of culture comprised of a series of 'significant' thinkers from
philosophical, literary critical and humanist schools of thought,
for example, Bentham, Coleridge, Arnold, Carlyle, Lawrence,
Tawney, Eliot and Orwell; not all of whom he regards as sympathetic. He then attempted a dialectical realization of their ideas
as a response to, but also as emanating from the material circumstances and turbulent and even violent change induced through
industrialization and capitalism within the civil society. By implication the thesis also addresses the changes engendered by the
French Revolution within the political society, but, as Williams
was later to admit, his early work was very much concerned with
the idea of culture within the English tradition, so this element
is somewhat underplayed. It was, nevertheless, a formidable and
remarkable programme which has foreshadowed every subsequent excursion into the field of culture (including this slender
monograph). The idea of a 'long revolution' for Williams was
intended to capture the narrative running throughout his writings
on culture; it reaffirmed his unequivocal sense of culture as process, rather than stasis, and as evolving positively rather than as
eroding. He asserted the primacy of cultural production in social
life, an idea not always well received by traditional Marxism, and
addressed the transitions of modernity through three systems, the
'democratic', the 'industrial' and the 'cultural', not all of which
are causally driven by the economic base. Williams comes to
place a particular emphasis on the 'creative mind' as an emergent
and critical condition of being and shows its positioning in relation
to the social and political history of mass education, mass literacy,
mass media in the form of the press, and drama. In the course of
this critique of the base/superstructure form of analysis Williams
further enters into dispute with the conceived nature of economic
activity though the development of capitalism. Instead of regarding the economy as a system of production he treats it rather as
a system of maintenance; this formulation points us away from
the more simplistic and reductionist views of economy as subsistence towards the concept of the economy existing as one part

of the complex network of control that pertains in advanced capitalism.

Despite these apparently wilful breaks with the basic tenets of historical materialism Williams persists in his views that any socialist account of the history and development of culture is also an account of the history of class conflict; but he will not go as far as E. P. Thompson and regard it as the history of class struggle. This names particular and vital moments in the whole process for Williams. To this end he reaffirms his anthropological view of culture and directs us towards the gradual emergence of a common culture in Britain. He is not, then, forced into the position of citing a handful of working-class novelists, playwrights, poets and film makers as signs of the development of an oppositional proletarian culture. Further, within his conception of a complex of elements, rather than a totality, he espouses the view that at any particular historical period, and necessarily so, there are dominant, residual and emergent patterns of culture. His partial and relativist view of materialist explanations of cultural formations are well expressed when he states:

> If the art is a part of the society, there is no solid whole, outside it, to which, by the form of our question, we concede priority. The art is there, as an activity, with the production, the trading, the politics, the raising of families. To study the relations adequately we must study them actively, seeing all the activities as particular and contemporary forms of human energy. If we take any one of these activities, we can see how many of the others are reflected in it, in various ways according to the nature of the whole organization. . . . Thus art, while clearly related to the other activities, can be seen as expressing certain elements in the organization which, within that organization's terms could only have been expressed in this way. It is then not a question of relating the art to the society, but of studying all the activities and their interrelations, without any concession of priority to any one of them we may choose to abstract.[35]

There is an ambivalence in Williams's work between his elevation of culture to the status of central problematic in the progress towards democracy, an appropriate conceptualization for a materialist critique; and yet a decontextualizing of culture through a somewhat idealist hermeneutic. Culture is not special, it is mundane and part of everybody's everyday life; it is also conceived of as project, as change, as part of a proper and necessary human evolution and yet there is an essentialism in his work (as indeed there would have to be for an author to write a mini encyclopedia reducing culture to a finite set of 'Keywords'). The essentialism tends to depoliticize the very idea of culture and thus subvert the intended radicalism of his thesis. Williams is a Marxist who sees working-class culture as contributing to a 'common culture'. There is no sense of class antagonisms here but a communality and homeostasis that override the notion of contradiction. If culture can be classless then culture is no longer ideological. This being the case we are left with a benign and all-engrossing network of symbolic representations, a world of meanings, that are not amenable to the appropriation and reproduction of powerful and dominant groups who are seeking to legitimate their position in society.

> Art is necessary in order that man should be able to recognize and change the world. But art is also necessary by virtue of the magic in it.[36]

NOTES

[1] K. Marx, *Grundrisse der Kritik der Politischen Okonomie*, East Berlin (1953), p. 30.

[2] K. Marx, *Theses on Feuerbach*, London: Lawrence and Wishart (1970), p. 121.

[3] K. Marx, *The German Ideology*, London: Lawrence and Wishart (1970), p. 41.

[4] S. Avineri, *The Social and Political Thought of Karl Marx*, Cambridge: Cambridge University Press (1968).

[5] K. Marx, *The German Ideology*, op. cit., p. 47.

[6] K. Marx, *The German Ideology*, op. cit., p. 64–5.

[7] K. Marx, *The Poverty of Philosophy*, London: Lawrence and Wishart (1956), p. 100.

[8] Ibid., p. 105.

[9] G. Lichtheim, *Lukács*, London: Fontana (1970).

[10] G. Steiner, 'Georg Lukács and his Devil Pact', in *George Steiner – A Reader*, London: Pelican (1960), p. 67

[11] G. Lukács, *The Meaning of Contemporary Realism*, London: Merlin (1963), p. 48

[12] Ibid., p. 19.

[13] G. Lukács, *Writer and Critic*, London: Merlin Press (1970), p. 34.

[14] A. Swingewood, *Sociological Poetics and Aesthetic Theory*, London: Macmillan (1986), p. 60.

[15] G. Steiner, op. cit., p. 56.

[16] C. Boggs, *Gramsci's Marxism*, London: Pluto Press (1976), p. 12.

[17] A. Gramsci, 'Libero pensiero e penseiro libero', *Il Grido del Popolo* 15 June 1918: Scritti Giovanili (1971), p. 261.

[18] A. Gramsci, *Selections from the Prison Notebooks* (trans. and eds Q. Hoare and G. Nowell-Smith), London: Lawrence and Wishart (1973), pp. 404–5.

[19] Ibid., pp. 365–6.

[20] A. Gramsci, *Quaderni del Carcere*, Torino: Einaudi (1975), p. 638.

[21] A. Gramsci, *Selections from the Prison Notebooks*, op. cit., p. 161.

[22] Ibid, p. 9.

[23] Ibid, p. 10.

[24] L. Goldmann, *The Hidden God*, London: Routledge & Kegan Paul (1964), p. 269.

[25] Ibid., p. 15.

[26] Ibid., p. 17.

[27] A. Swingewood, op. cit., p. 117.

[28] L. Goldmann, 'La Reification', in *Recherches dialectiques* (trans. M. Evans), Paris: Gallimard (1959), p. 96.

[29] W. Benjamin, *Gesammelte Schriften* (ed. R. Tiedermann), Frankfurt: Suhrkamp (1982), p. 677.

[30] R. Wolin, *Walter Benjamin: An Aesthetic of Redemption*, New York (1982), pp. 187–8 (quoted in D. Frisby, *Fragments of Modernity*, Cambridge: Polity [1985]).

[31] W. Benjamin, op. cit., p. 51.

[32] W. Benjamin, *Illuminations*, London: Cape (1970), p. 190.

[33] A. Swingewood, op. cit., p. 83.

[34] R. Williams, *Politics and Letters*, London: NLB (1979), p. 98.

[35] R. Williams, *The Long Revolution*, Harmondsworth: Penguin (1965), p. 61–2.

[36] E. Fischer, *The Necessity of Art: A Marxist Approach*, Harmondsworth: Penguin (1963).

5

Cultural stratification

In a strong sense cultural stratification is not an exclusive category, and it is certainly not a well-insulated category, as a whole variety of notions of stratification permeate all of our discussions of the concept of 'culture'. Throughout this current work we have repeatedly confronted the distinction between the idea of high culture as belonging to a privileged group and the idea of culture being that which defines the whole way of life of a people and we shall, no doubt, rehearse this distinction again. However there are many other dimensions, differentiations, hierarchies and rankings through which we might discuss this idea of cultural stratification, just as is the case in reference to an understanding of the totality of social life. These distinctions are no trivial matter; in each instance they divide lives and provide the grounds for contest. Let us look at a few important examples.

We have already considered the relationship between the ideas of culture and social structure, and a large part of that discussion centred around the chronological development of social and cultural anthropology and the theoretical frameworks that accompanied their, often highly competitive and contentious, explanations of the cultural process. What can get left behind in such a debate between schools of thought is, not so much the intellectual, but rather the social and political relationship between the discipline and its phenomena. If we adopt the relatively crude view that early anthropology constituted the superstructure of western colonialism then we can regard their classifying and collecting ethnographies as forays in sampling the scarce resources of other cultures, and their expansive, and largely functionalist, theories as the imperialist market research into the power structures and systems of control of the Third World. Now all of this emotive language is not meant as a simple indictment of the political incorrectness of anthropology's past but rather to point to the clear sense of superiority, emanating from an ideology of 'development', that prefigured the intellectually predatory western mind. The sense of stratification we have at work here then, is that taken-for-granted relation between the First World and the Third World, the developed and the underdeveloped, the complex and the simple, the advanced and the backward, the literate and the traditional. This is both the conscious and unconscious stratification to which Freire refers when he states that:

> Cultural conquest leads to the cultural inauthenticity of those who are invaded; they begin to respond to the values, the standards and the goals of the invaders. . . . For cultural invasion to succeed, it is essential that those invaded become convinced of their intrinsic inferiority. . . . Cultural invasion is on the one hand an *instrument* of domination, and on the other, the *result* of domination. Thus, cultural action of a dominating character, in addition to being deliberate and planned, is in another sense simply a product of oppressive reality.[1]

This is the corrosive, but now itself eroding, form of stratification that Fanon highlights in his own acerbic way when he tells us that 'To believe that it is possible to create a black culture, is to forget that niggers are disappearing, just as those people who brought them into being are seeing the break-up of their economic and cultural supremacy'.[2] And this is the methodological stratification which Frank attacks in his essay which

> . . . examines the sociology of development currently being produced in the developing countries, especially the United States, for export to and use in the under-

developed countries. On critical examination, this new
sociology of development is found to be empirically
invalid when confronted with reality, theoretically inadequate in terms of its own classical social scientific standards, and policy wise ineffective for pursuing its
supposed intentions of promoting the development of the
underdeveloped countries. Furthermore, the inadequacy
grows along with the development of the society which
produces it. Like the underdeveloped society to which it
is applied, this sociology is becoming increasingly underdeveloped.[3]

In part overlapping with the stratification of culture that arises
from the ideologies of imperialism are those forms of stratification
which seem persistently to emerge from the experiences of race
and ethnicity. As modern western societies have become increasingly multi-racial and multi-ethnic, if only by description rather
than through any practice of real 'equality' or 'pluralism', then
so also have these categories provided new grounds for differentiation and stratification. What is important here is the collective
recognition of racial status characteristics, treated as natural, and
their articulation in terms of the collective behavioural patterns
and symbolic representations of ethnicity, real or supposed, that
are treated as cultural. As will be seen in more detail in Chapter
9, issues of race and ethnicity are easily, and conveniently, conflated and left embedded in the sentiments and politics of both
liberalism and reaction. Melting pots and ghettos, integration and
isolation, multiculturalism and cultural integrity provide for a
battery of problems that are not simply analytic in character.
Ideologies of racism, supremacy, purity and cleansing are all
available for scrutiny in the assessment of cultural stratification,
whether through their formulation of negative racial stereotypes
or through the very invisibility of race that they seem to project;
in theory, just as in 'polite' conversation. We did not require
George Steiner to inform us that the cultures of the world will
never be the same again after Auschwitz, except that we do,
every day, as nobody seems to have heard.

Our final example, and one concerning perhaps the most
successful voice to have projected itself forward into the arena of
cultural analysis, is the cultural stratification that occurs through
gender. This is not a 'discovery' parallel with the recognition of
women's difference within the division of labour by the sociology

of advanced industrial societies, or simply a necessary comple-
ment to the rhetoric of feminist activism. The issue of gender
stratification within culture can be applied equally to the spectrum
of polysexuality. A culture, as a process, proliferates with artefacts, customs, symbolic representations and conventions which
appear, on the surface, to be applicable to and generated by all
people who inhabit that culture. However, Spender informs us
that 'man made language', her thesis being that the most fundamental of all shared aspects of being human, language itself,
contains, in terms of its performance, vocabulary and syntax, a
series of deep structural buttresses to male domination. Goffman
offers us an analysis of sexual stereotype images in the mass
communication of gender advertisements; Dworkin provides an
account of the centrality of pornography to male/female relationships; Sydie generates an appraisal of the natural 'culturedness'
of masculinity and the cultured 'naturalness' of femininity;[4] and
McRobbie puts forward an examination of the 'invisibility' of
women in cultural studies:

> There have been studies of the relation of male youth to
> class and class culture, to the machinery of the State,
> and to the school, community and workplace. Football
> has been analyzed as a male sport, drinking as a male
> form of leisure, the law and the police as patriarchal
> structures concerned with young male (potential)
> offenders. I don't know of a study that considers, never
> mind prioritises, youth and the family; women and the
> whole question of sexual division have been marginal-
> ised.[5]

This handful of contributions to the field in no way exhausts the
vast and growing body of literature relevant to the issue of gender
and culture,[6] nor do the concepts of 'patriarchy', 'marginalization'
and 'stereotyping' exhaust its critique; however, we are pointing
towards a significant and increasingly public dimension of cultural
stratification. The predominant social division through which cultural stratification is effected and on which this account will, by
choice, concentrate is that of social class. There are no societies
in which the quality of life is not differentiated by complexes of
class, status and power, and as societies become more complex
this differentiation becomes more marked, but also more subtly
encoded in networks of symbolic cultural representations. For a
variety of reasons western, and particularly European, culture

has come to order its people alongside their capacity for understanding. Perhaps following the Aristotelian legacy of true knowledge being the knowledge of ultimate causes, a conflation has occurred between truth and quality, and reason and judgement. The purpose of being is to know, knowing is regulated by the truth, and not all people have an equivalent relation to this goal. When enjoined with a 'polis' named democracy, which is functionally a benevolent oligarchy, we have the historical grounds for a culture that is stratified intrinsically in terms of its very texture, and stratified extrinsically in terms of the appropriate characteristics of the guardians of that texture.

F. R. LEAVIS: SOCIO-LITERARY THOUGHT AND THE ORGANIC COMMUNITY

F. R. Leavis, writing in 1930 in a pamphlet called *Mass Civilization and Minority Culture*, which was often to be quoted as summarizing his position on culture, states the following:

> In any period it is upon a very small minority that the discerning appreciation of art and literature depends: it is (apart from cases of the simple and familiar) only a few who are capable of unprompted, first-hand judgement. They are still a small minority, though a larger one, who are capable of endorsing such first-hand judgement by genuine personal response. . . . The minority capable not only of appreciating Dante, Shakespeare, Baudelaire, Hardy (to take major instances) but of recognising their latest successors constitute the consciousness of the race (or of a branch of it) at a given time. . . . Upon this minority depends our power of profiting by the finest human experience of the past; they keep alive the subtlest and most perishable parts of the tradition. Upon them depend the implicit standards that order the finer living of an age, the sense that it is worth more than that, this rather than that is the direction in which to go. In their keeping . . . is the language, the changing idiom upon which fine living depends, and without which distinction of spirit is thwarted and incoherent. By 'culture' I mean the use of such language.[7]

Leavis was a leading figure in a school of British academics for whom the study of English and the practice of literary criticism was regarded as a path to the good life, enlightenment, the very core of all that is pure and worthy in the human condition and a panacea for the wasting condition that afflicted society as a whole. A previous professor of English Literature had stated that:

> England is sick, and . . . English literature must save it. The Churches (as I understand) having failed, and social remedies being slow, English literature has now a triple function: still, I suppose, to delight and instruct us, but also, and above all, to save our souls and heal the State.[8]

But Leavis was no eccentric, esoteric, other-worldly figure; his ideas picked up very much on the spirit of the time. Following in the lineage of Arnold and other of the literary-Romantic figures that we discussed in Chapter 1, there was a persistent and nagging strain among the intelligentsia, radically opposed to the ravages perpetrated through the so-called progress of industrialization. This strain had been further exacerbated, in the early twentieth century, by the four years of horror and 'rational' and 'mechanical' waste of the First World War.

The monumental trivializing and pain, in direct proportion, that had accompanied the *fin de siècle* had generated an inverted historical optimism. Whereas the conventional post-Enlightenment rhetoric seems to run that what is cannot be the best, we must anticipate and hasten the next stage of our cultural evolution, what was now afoot was a grand longing for times past. As with all avowals of 'the good old days' the actual historical circumstances are more imagined than real and more amenable to introspection than the disruptions of actual change. The 'organic community' of Leavis's fantasies and recollections was an unspecific seventeenth-century England when clearly civilization had reached its zenith in an integration of the head and the heart, the eye and the mind, and the natural and the cultural.

> It is on literary tradition that the office of maintaining continuity must rest. . . . What we have lost is the organic community with the living culture it embodied. Folk-songs, folk-dances, Cotswold cottages and handi-craft products are a sign of something more: an art of life, a way of living, ordered and patterned, involving social arts, codes of intercourse and a responsive adjust-ment, growing out of immemorial experience, to the

natural environment and the rhythm of the year. . . .
The machine has destroyed the old ways of life, the old
forms, and by reason of the continuous rapid change it
involves, prevented the growth of the new.[9]

Given, in some way, that this idyll could not be recaptured by
the many, it was to become the destiny and the purpose of the
few.

Leavis was, for almost a decade, locked in a debate with C.
P. Snow,[10] whose thesis was that far from there being one core
culture that modernity had obscured there were, in fact, two, the
literary-artistic and the scientific, the creation of the latter being
a specific triumph of modernity. These two spheres of knowledge
were distinct but equivalent, and integral to the educated person;
an ignorance of contemporary physics was comparable to an
ignorance of Shakespeare. Apart from the fact that analytically
this challenged Leavis's view that a shared culture resided in a
shared language, 'a language is a life', Snow had an implicit
preference for the scientific culture and populist support in terms
of the new vocationalism. The debate was extremely antagonistic,
and divided whole sixth forms across the land; 'aesthetes' drew
up lines against the 'barbarous' scientists, but the latter inherited
the earth (and very nearly destroyed it). Though delicate and
appealing, at a series of levels, there is no danger of mistaking
the message in Leavis through the intricacies of interpretation
and irony. Social life is not to be regarded as an experience that
is, either demonstrably or purposively, similar for all people.
People are marked out by their intellect and their capacity for
discriminating judgement, they are differentiated according to
this yardstick and they appropriately group in relation to this
essential sign of difference. The 'third realm', which is for Leavis
the realm of sociality, '. . . the collaboratively created human
world, the realm of what is neither public . . . nor merely private', is a world extending from the sphere of common culture
to that of minority culture, sundered by modernity but potentially
mediated through language, art and literature and criticism, and
to be bound by the literary tradition, 'such a tradition as repre-
sents the finer consciousness of the race . . . and provides the
currency of finer living', and the cultural tradition, 'in all things
standards above the level of the ordinary man'. The free
unspecialized general intelligence must transcend its time, and
the mass, and locate the good in tradition. A centre of excellence

must hold, 'for the good of all of us' and the discerning elite will radiate and disperse around this centre. Privilege requires its binary opposition deprivation, just as minority culture gains its distinction in opposition to the culture of the masses. Great literature captures essential elements of human experience, manifests individual authors and elicits creative personal readers. This stands in opposition to the products of mass culture, ironically applauded by Benjamin, which are produced collectively, anonymously, commercially and without creative elan. The latter reflect the mechanical materiality of their time not the essence of human experience; they can be neither good nor liberating.

The reunification of society, through culture, Leavis recommends, will occur through a considered programme of liberal education. Such a programme will enable a strong educated public who will reclaim the most vital features of social, political and moral life.

> Thus the public in its totality will represent that strong living sense of complexities which is needed, above all in a time of rapid change, to ensure that the achievements, spiritual and humane – the essential creative achievements – of our civilization shall be permanent gains, conserved in the cultural heritage.[11]

Leavis's ideas, disseminated through his extensive writings, his teaching and his formulation of critical debate through the journal *Scrutiny*, had a considerable impact on cultural criticism both during his time and subsequently. So also have those of his Cambridge contemporary, T. S. Eliot.

T. S. ELIOT: TRADITION AND THE ELITE

Eliot's influence upon the thinking of the English-speaking world is extensive. Recognized, perhaps primarily, as a literary critic and highly successful poet, his work extended into cultural and social theory and, in Britain after the Second World War, impacted onto politics and educational policy. His primary thesis concerns the necessarily stratified and non-democratic character of culture.

Born and initially educated in America, he trained as a philosopher, became a friend of Bertrand Russell despite the political chasm that separated their thoughts, and was much influenced by the neo-Hegelian metaphysics of F. H. Bradley. Fired by this radical idealism, and the preoccupation with searching out the absolute reality behind the superficiality of appearances he was led to a commitment to 'essence', in the various forms of the 'good', 'cultural heritage', 'tradition', and, in parallel, a Christian God.

Eliot's most important works in the area of cultural criticism are *After Strange Gods*, *The Idea of a Christian Society* and *Notes Towards the Definition of Culture*; these were published between the years 1934 and 1949 and demonstrate the evolution of his views on the malaise of modernity and its resolution in a return to the structures of social life in a world past. The form of his own literary creations was imaginative and notable for its innovation, yet he was opposed to the unlocated and ill-disciplined drives of modernism as a project; he announced that the search was on for a fecund and unifying European literary tradition. He had, at an earlier stage of his career, pointed to a moment in cultural history where a serious decline in value had been instigated. The classicism of the pre-seventeenth century had become fragmented through a dislocation of cognition and affect, what Eliot referred to as the 'dissociation of sensibilities'; the 'essence' had been lost and modernisms now dispersed into private languages and bizarre and particularistic imagery. The prophet, the seeker after truth, the creative artist must now resurrect the monotheism of a shared tradition of value that the process of culture must properly coalesce around. Eliot was such a prophet.

For Eliot, the breakdown of a concerted literary and artistic tradition was no mere esoteric occurrence, affecting only the small band of practising artists, critics and surrounding aesthetes; the breakdown, as it instanced the loss of an essential good, threatened the whole way of life of the people. The state of the creative project was thus realized as index of the state of the collective consciousness in the wider society. Modern society is thus marked by a lack of shared values and beliefs, and an increasing failure to achieve shared meanings; the language and the very system of communication at the core of the culture are steadily corroding. This belief leads Eliot to contradict the conventional wisdom of modernist aesthetics which stresses creativity through difference, newness and fracture. He, in opposition, locates the creative artist in the practice of the recovery, redemption and salvation of the tradition that grounds the possibility of recognizable cultural production. So consolidation and roots appear to be the goal. The reconstitution of a literary tradition is also a moral project, for Eliot, almost in the way of a Durkheimian sociologist seeking out the appropriate creed to ensure a solidaristic community in the face of material changes and pressures on the structuring of relationships. Paradoxically, he also sees many of the evils of modern society being manifested in the kind of representations that Marx had previously polemicized: the competitive ethic engendered through capitalism, the organization of human relationships in terms of the discourse of the market place, the central motif of commerce as mediating all social life, the fetishism of commodities, the exploitation of human beings in the form of labour, and the election of profit as the primary motive in social action. All of these guiding principles of modern culture and modern social life run counter to the moral Christian life; just as they had previously affronted Marx's residual Judaism.

In *Notes Towards the Definition of Culture* Eliot finally reveals his somewhat less than egalitarian views about the necessary stratification of cultural experience and socialization. He presents the case, initially, as if it concerned levels of analysis but these levels take on a more positive form and become justifications for levels of participation and the quality of experience. The three cultural strata are the individual, the group and the whole society. We cannot and, he affirms, should not, elect standards at any one of these levels and render them applicable to any of the other levels; thus, particular individuals can only achieve, culturally, at the level of particular individuals. As a consequence it is wholly inappropriate to attempt to educate the majority into the culture of the minority. This leads instantly to a conflation of the notions of high culture and minority culture. The attempted democratization of high culture leads to a dilution and a falling off of standards. The 'essence', the quality and tradition at the centre of a culture in general must, for the good of all, be preserved by the guardians of our aesthetic heritage; an argument reminiscent of Plato's *Republic*.

Although the ritual, routine and convention of our shared cultural way of life are practices upheld by all members of a society, unconsciously in their everyday lives, there is a particular necessity for the excellences and pinnacles of cultural achievement to be sustained consciously. This is the peculiar responsibility of an elite, and not a spontaneous or organic elite that emerges according to the dominant material circumstances of the day. Our cultural heritage, our creative tradition requires nurture through continuity which is, itself, best provided through the maintenance of the class system (which is the form in which modernity and capitalism have come to express and institutionalize meritocracy). This recommendation we might read as an apologia for the system of inherited 'cultural capital' that we will later see indicted in the work of Bourdieu.

ORTEGA Y GASSET: THE THREAT OF THE MASSES

Outside this seemingly English, all too English, strand of elitist cultural criticism there existed a steady and consolidated body of American reactionary cultural analysis which, quite independently of Marcuse, was fearful of what it variously conceived as the 'one-dimensionality' of human expression and desire that appeared to follow in the wake of the exponentially, all-consuming popular culture. Such ideas, in the American context, further amplified the then current McCarthyite trend in politics, the terror of socialist 'uniformity'.

In isolation from this debate, yet latterly informing it with a sharp philosophical clarity, was the forceful and prolific writing of Spanish philosopher Ortega y Gasset working in Madrid up until 1955. His interests covered a wide span including aesthetics, metaphysics, logic, existentialism and cultural life. His unequivocal ideas on cultural stratification appear quite spontaneous until we discover that having received a German university education he became much influenced by neo-Kantianism. His social theorizing asserts the absolute fragility and volatility of culture. Whereas Thomas Hobbes, some centuries earlier, had seen the resolution to social instability residing in the overwhelming and overseeing power of the State, his 'Leviathan', Ortega y Gasset envisages this role being taken over by a select and cultured aristocratic group. For Hobbes, the perpetual and challenging alternative to social order was an anarchy involving a war of all against all; for Ortega y Gasset the disassembly of cultural stability would be marked by a descent into barbarianism and a lethargy of the human spirit. Not all of humanity is sufficiently equipped, or indeed interested, to guard the heritage of quality that constitutes human culture, and thus the constant vigilance that is required to resist cultural and moral decay is to be provided through the leadership of a cultural elite, albeit a liberal cultural elite. The part of the common man, who is unable to provide the necessary energy and insight to police his own culture, is to acquiesce to the leadership of the elite.

> Because the being of man is not given to him but is a purely imaginary possibility, the human species is of an instability and variability that make it incomparable with animal species. Men are enormously unequal, in spite of what egalitarians of the last two centuries affirmed and of what old-fashioned folk of this century go on affirming.[12]

We can hear echoes of Nietzsche here, another influence on the work of Ortega y Gasset, who had already announced that if you had a culture that required slaves then it was not sensible to educate them to become masters. This anti-democratic sentiment is adequately summarized in the title of Ortega y Gasset's major contribution to the argument over mass culture, *The Revolt of the Masses* (1930). For him the tendency towards the social, collective and popular response, inherent in the dense sociality of the industrial world, is a tendency towards the subhuman and the mechanized. Mass society and mass culture, clearly now political rather than descriptive terms, are threats to the expressive and creative project of human being. The social and the cultural do not hold together through spontaneous, egalitarian loving bonds but through the continuous, wilful and dedicated project of the informed minority working for the destiny of all.

Far from recognizing any commonality with the tradition of Marxist theorizing expounded in Chapter 4, Leavis and Eliot and Ortega y Gasset have been seen as reactionary, theorists of the 'right', and worse. Their position is linked with other, manifestly conservative, thinkers such as Jacques Ellul, Ernest van den Haag and Russell Kirk. It is nevertheless the case that there is a surprising degree of overlap between some of their ideas on aesthetics and tradition and cultural representation, and those ideas of the group of German critical theorists that we have come to collect as the Frankfurt School. Clearly the spirit of the time temporarily overwhelmed existing political differences.

THE FRANKFURT SCHOOL: MASS CULTURE AND THE 'CULTURE INDUSTRY'

It is, in many ways, one of the grand paradoxes and ironies of contemporary social theory that a concerted, prolific and radical group of Marxist scholars should have constituted a thesis on the character, value and function of mass culture that is personified by condemnation rather than redemption. Nevertheless, the 'critical theory' of Adorno, Horkheimer, Lowenthal and Marcuse has made a lasting, left-wing platform for the espousal of the critique of mass culture and thus the inevitable stratification of culture. The irony of this forcefully argued theme in their work is no less bitter than that engendered by the image of the windows in the Frankfurt Institute, broken by the student revolutionaries of 1968. A melancholy science indeed.

Before we look specifically at the ideas of the Frankfurt School it is important to note their dissimilarities from the positions of the conservative critics, previously discussed. The conservatives are clearly opposed to egalitarianism whereas the critical theorists are committed to political democracy. This difference is based on antagonistic views of the people and their intrinsic worth; thus the conservative explanation of the paucity of mass culture is in relation to the inadequacy, mundanity and 'low-brow' status of the general public's taste and receptive capacities – the Marxist explanation is in terms of the intervention of the market, and the erosion of spontaneous folk-culture in the face of a mechanical and commercially exploitative popular culture imposed outside the control of the volition of the masses. Both groups of critics remain, however, disturbed, if not threatened, by the rise of an increasingly autonomous and, as they see it, vacuous popular culture.

During the 1930s in its striving to explain the distortion of both the individual personality and the collective response that occurred through totalitarianism, the Frankfurt School supplanted the search for an economic base in their theorizing with an allegiance to psychology and psychoanalysis. This involved a sustained dalliance with the system of Freudian ideas, but largely through the mediation of Reich and Fromm. This shift from the level of the social to that of the individual, indeed to the inner self, was a sincere attempt to relate to the dramatic transformations in human conduct that routinely took place as a result of the calculated 'manipulations' of fascist propaganda. Gentle folk became mass murderers and previously unremarkable differences in race and ethnicity became 'reasonable' grounds for denunciation and extermination. Manifestly, this was no passing interest; the members of the Institute had, themselves, to escape to the USA in order to avoid the inevitable consequences of the manipulated Nazi hysteria that had metamorphosed into a rational machine for the constitution of a 'pure' future and a purged history.

In the USA, the haven from the mass phenomenon of persecution, the members of the Institute confronted their new phenomenon, which was to provide further impetus to the pursuit of a theory of 'manipulation'. America pulsated with an advanced form of capitalism, unprecedented and unchallenged in the western world. Here was no fascism, but a society with relationships regulated by the rules of a market economy, motivated by the drives of possessive individualism, orientated towards ownership and achievement and, most important, socialized, massaged and informed by an equally manipulative popular culture.

It seemed no longer relevant to account for the origins of the 'authoritarian personality' in terms of poor toilet training or an inadequate repression of libidinal urges. What they looked towards now was the complex conflation of entertainment, leisure, advertising, commerce, lifestyle and mass media that generated the 'one-dimensional' American 'man': and this complex Adorno and Horkheimer referred to as the 'culture industry'. The study of psychology moved to a critique of mass culture.

This analysis of 'enlightenment as mass deception' is a new, and truly sociological, departure in the work of the Frankfurt School. As Bottomore has described it,

> The argument deployed here is not that of Marx, according to which 'the ruling ideas in every age are the ideas of the ruling class' and modern technology might be regarded as having increased the effectiveness with which these ideas are implanted in society at large (a hypothesis to be tested by empirical studies), but rather that technology and a technological consciousness have themselves produced a new phenomenon in the shape of a uniform and debased 'mass culture' which aborts and silences criticism.[13]

There is a sad, if not tragic, vision informing the School's work of this period. The 'culture industry' is not just a description of the capitalist mechanisms of manipulation and Fordist cultural production, it is a concept containing a whole way of life, indeed the state of being of the working classes. The term 'mass culture' is virtually replaced by the notion of a 'culture industry' in the work of Adorno and Horkheimer; it sums up not an apparatus imposed by outside forces of exploitation, but a wholly integrated lifestyle and a wholly predictable and replicable course of action for this great body of the people. The vision here is one of fallenness and it is understood with a profound pessimism.

Marx's proletariat, the historical vehicle for revolutionary social change, the group previously endowed with a transformative latency (whatever the state of its oppressive structural conditions), the immanent potential for activism whose destiny it is to cast off the chains that constrain human possibility and expunge the violence of any status quo; this proletariat has become utterly routinized. It has transmogrified into passivity and complacency, and its will to power has diminished if not withered. The proletariat is no longer a revolutionary force.

The Frankfurt School had escaped a tidal wave of European fascism to become engulfed in a stagnant pool of decadence and, to invoke their own term, 'barbarity'. Their realization of the apathetic and malleable condition of the American populace could not, however, be explained through some version of a 'culture shock' theory; this was a view supported in perhaps more vociferous fashion by the endogenous Marxist sociologist C. Wright Mills whose work on *The Power Elite* (1956) argued that there had been an almost total collapse in civil society and that political life was now constituted through a more or less direct relation between a self-selected and manipulative 'them' and a mass and manipulable 'us'. The political context further inflamed the viability of the thesis in that the previous McCarthyite fears of uniformity wrought through the machinations of the 'red' peril now, by virtue of the war in Korea, shifted to the propaganda of the 'yellow' peril with talk of mind control and 'brain washing'. The 'masses' were abandoned, within the theory, to the strategies of the 'hidden persuaders'. They were left to consume their pulp fiction, ubiquitous and continuous television, drive-in movies, fast food, addictive comics, radio that 'entertained' but never informed; in fact, a life at the prey of advertising.

Horkheimer and Adorno's *Dialectic of Enlightenment* is an analysis of the 'culture industry' but it is also the cry of despair of aesthetic Marxism, now off in pursuit of a site for culture in the more traditional, high cultural forms of *Kultur*. The culture industry, Swingewood tells us,

> . . . was clearly intended to suggest domination from above although its success still depended on an amorph-

ous, passive and irrational working class. The mass media are repressive: criticism of capitalism is stifled, happiness is identified with acquiescence and with the complete integration of the individual into the existing social and political order. Two themes dominate the Frankfurt School's theory of mass society: the weakness of traditional socialising institutions in the face of massive economic and technological change; and the increasing reification of culture in which the object of man's labour and activity are transformed into independent, autonomous forces seemingly beyond human control.[14]

The collapse of the family, or rather the erosion of its role as socializer of the rational, choosing autonomous individual, had vacated the space now occupied by the 'culture industry'. Thus the 'home of the free and the brave' had now become the receptacle of Marcuse's 'one-dimensional man'.

From Horkheimer's analysis of the family and the structure of authority the Frankfurt School proceeded to find salvation for the human condition and its cultural manifestations in the traditional repositories of free, genuine art, and the free, genuine, creative consciousness of the artist. This may be an antidote to the oppression of mass culture but it never has been, and never could be, a propensity of more than the 'few'. There is no new proletariat here. The Frankfurt School have moved from a critical appraisal of cultural stratification to a justification of cultural stratification.

POPULAR CULTURE: A POSITIVE APPRAISAL – CULTURAL PLURALISM

What we have noted throughout this chapter is that mass or popular culture is realized, analytically, as the antithesis and inferior partner of high culture. It is one of those concepts that conventionally inhabits the shadows, like deviance, such that one begins to relate to it, from the outset, as constitutionally deprived, belonging to the less-than-good, or at least as signifying other than 'good' taste. Although Williams, from a Marxist perspective, may have pointed to the design and construction of trade union banners, for example, as instances of working-class art and creative pursuit he nevertheless demonstrates a certain ambivalence in treating them as equivalent to or competitive with what we all know as 'fine' art. It is indeed a brave, or ambitious, theorist who will go as far as to flaunt 'informed' public opinion and declare the intrinsic worth of Paul McCartney's music alongside that of Bach, Catherine Cookson's prose in tandem with Proust, or the painting of David Hockney adjacent to Cézanne (the distinction begins to blur . . .) but what we have to address here is not an argument concerning absolute standards set by gods or philosophers, but rather an argument over the sociological significance of the performance and reception of these various manifestations of culture. This point provides an important political stance for much of contemporary British cultural studies, as we shall see in Chapter 8; it had, however, been previously addressed by theorists such as Gans[15] and Gerbner[16] and others in America, such as Shils, Bell and Riesmann in the 1950s through to the early 1970s.

> A new order of society has taken form since the end of World War I in the United States. . . . The new society is a mass society precisely in the sense that the mass of the population has become incorporated *into* society. The centre of society – the central institutions and the central value systems which guide and legitimate these institutions – has extended its boundaries. Most of the population (the 'mass') now stands in a closer relationship to the centre than has been the case either in premodern societies or in the earlier phases of modern society.[17]

The argument runs that modern society, through changes in its productive base and demographic distributions, has experienced a significant shift in the character of its class system, a strengthening of its civil society and an increased incorporation of the populace through notions of citizenship. All people, within the post-industrial society, have more freedom, more choice, and clearly, more self-expression. Popular culture then is not simply an exercise in exploitation or mechanical reproduction but instead it fulfils a need and a desire of a particular, but genuine, kind of taste or tastes. Beyond this, given the transitory and historically located character of experience, all people have a right, and now the autonomy, to choose the cultural representations that they prefer. Adopting this kind of position Gans tells us that the critique of popular culture is misplaced and consists of four elements, being:

1.   *The negative character of popular culture creation*. Popular culture is desirable because, unlike high culture, it is mass-produced by profit-minded entrepreneurs solely for the gratification of a paying audience.

2.   *The negative effects on high culture*. Popular culture borrows from high culture, thus debasing it, and also lures away many potential creators of high culture, thus depleting its reservoir of talent.

3.   *The negative effects on the popular cultural audience*. The consumption of popular culture content at best produces spurious gratifications, and at worst is emotionally harmful to the audience.

4.   *The negative effects on the society*. The wide distribution of popular culture not only reduces the level of cultural quality – or civilization – of a society, but also encourages totalitarianism by creating a passive audience peculiarly responsive to the techniques of mass persuasion used by demagogues bent on dictatorship.[18]

These four theses rest, however, on a set of interests that are particular and biased. Cultural populism, in juxtaposition, is a hard argument to make given that most of the potential presenters would, themselves, be appreciators of high culture and thus at risk, at the very least, of patronage. Nevertheless a truly democratic argument in favour of popular culture recognizes not its value in signifying the state of its times, as an abstraction unidentifiable by its consumers, but its worth as supplying a taste, awareness and a set of desires that belong to a people.

Gans, arguing in favour of such pluralism, suggests that the critique is biased and misplaced in a variety of ways. Initially, there is no evidence to suggest that popular culture contains the harmful attributes with which it is ascribed. All cultural representations live in a peaceful, if not symbiotic, co-existence. The critique, he says, is largely ideological, it rests upon an aesthetic rejection of the content of popular culture and a 'disdain for ordinary people'. More than this, it embodies a regressive view of the historical process, a bourgeois and Enlightenment view of individualism, and is clearly creator, rather than consumer, oriented. However, Gans and the other cultural pluralists retain the distinction between the mass, or popular, culture and the high, or minority, culture; and also the distinction between the 'ordinary' people and, presumably, the more-than-ordinary people. More than this, they gloss over the central concerns of the two modes of theorizing that they seek to resolve by ignoring all questions of cultural value and vitality, and also those of exploitation and domination.

> The theory of pluralism . . . has a concept of modern society based on an equilibrium of forces in which independent, non-inclusive social groups exercise a limited measure of democratic control through their access to the major elites. Society is thus a complex structure of checks and balances in which no one group wields dominant power. . . . Consumer capitalism, rather than creating a vast, homogeneous and culturally brutalised mass, generates different levels of taste, different audiences and consumers. Culture is stratified, its consumption differentiated.[19]

It is left until 1977 for Swingewood in *The Myth of Mass Culture* to produce a synthesis and critique of the conservative position, the Frankfurt School and the cultural pluralists, and to announce that all three groups of theorists are involved in the perpetuation of a political myth, that of 'mass culture'. Mass culture is not just a descriptive category, it is a rhetorical weapon in a series of arguments variously augmenting cultural stratification based on social class.

NOTES

[1] P. Freire, *The Pedagogy of the Oppressed*, Harmondsworth: Penguin (1972), pp. 122–3.

[2] F. Fanon, *The Wretched of the Earth*, Paris: Presence Africaine (1963), p. 188.

[3] A. G. Frank, *Sociology of Development and Underdevelopment of Sociology*, London: Pluto Press (1971), p. 2.

[4] D. Spender, *Man Made Language*, London: Routledge & Kegan Paul (1980); I. Goffman, *Gender Advertisements*, London: Macmillan (1979); A. Dworkin, *Pornography*, New York: Pedigree Books (1981); R. A. Sydie, *Natural Women, Cultured Men*, Milton Keynes: Open University Press (1987).

[5] A. McRobbie, 'Settling accounts with subcultures: a feminist critique', in T. Bennett, *Culture, Ideology and Social Process*, London: Batsford (1981), p. 111 (a view not wholly

dissimilar to that of P. Gilroy, *There Ain't No Black in the Union Jack*, London: Hutchinson [1987] on the 'invisibility' of race).

[6] See R. Billington, S. Strawbridge, L. Greensides and A. Fitzsimons, *Culture and Society*, London: Macmillan (1991), Ch. 7.

[7] F. R. Leavis, *Mass Civilization and Minority Culture*, Cambridge: The Minority Press (1930), pp. 3–5.

[8] G. Gordon, 'Inaugural Lecture; Oxford University', quoted in T. Eagleton, *Literary Theory*, Oxford: Blackwell (1983), p. 23.

[9] F. R. Leavis and D. Thompson, *Culture and Environment*, London: Chatto and Windus (1933), p. 23.

[10] C. P. Snow, *The Two Cultures and A Second Look*, Cambridge: Cambridge University Press (1970).

[11] F. R. Leavis, *'Nor Shall My Sword': Discourses on Pluralism, Compassion and Social Hope*, Chatto and Windus (1972), p. 227.

[12] J. Ortega y Gasset, *Meditación de la Técnica*, Madrid (1933), p. 42.

[13] T. Bottomore, *The Frankfurt School*, London: Tavistock (1984), p. 19.

[14] A. Swingewood, *The Myth of Mass Culture*, London: Macmillan (1977), p. 13.

[15] H. J. Gans, *Popular Culture and High Culture*, New York: Basic Books (1974).

[16] G. Gerbner, O. Holsti, K. Krippendorff, W. Paisley and P. Stone, *The Analysis of Communication Content*, New York: John Wiley and Sons (1969).

[17] E. Shils, 'Mass society and its culture', in N. Jacobs (ed.), *Culture for the Millions*, Princeton, NJ: Van Nostrand (1961), p. 1.

[18] H. J. Gans, op. cit., p. 19.

[19] A. Swingewood, *The Myth of Mass Culture*, London: Macmillan (1977), pp. 19–20.

6

Cultural reproduction

Having gone some way towards establishing a working definition of the concept of culture, however volatile and transient, it is appropriate that we should attempt to account for both the recognition of change and the experience of consistency in our everyday relations with cultural formations. 'Cultural reproduction', though no longer the catch-all explanatory device that it once was, is nevertheless a useful analytic tool to this end and a particularly fertile area for social theory.[1] The idea of cultural reproduction makes reference to the emergent quality of the experience of everyday life, albeit through a variety of theoretical positions. The concept serves to articulate the dynamic process that makes sensible the utter contingency of, on the one hand, the stasis and determinacy of social structures and, on the other, the innovation and agency inherent in the practice of social action. Cultural reproduction allows us to contemplate the necessity and complementarity of continuity and change in social experience. To that end it both preserves the homeostasis between the elements of any semiotic system, such as culture, but also provides for the possibility, and inevitable nature, of its evolution.

While it might be argued that, in some senses, this particular problematic has been a sustained preoccupation of social theorizing since its inception, the modern critical conceptualization of the problem around the idea of 'cultural reproduction' was first developed by the French sociologist and cultural theorist Pierre Bourdieu in the early 1970s. The original practical context of Bourdieu's work was the modern system of education which he saw functioning to the end of 'reproducing' the culture of the dominant classes. Such a mechanism of mass socialization clearly assisted in ensuring this group's continued dominance and also in perpetuating their covert exercise of power.

ALTHUSSER: IDEOLOGICAL STATE APPARATUSES

Such ideas resonated with certain of Althusser's[2] concepts that were emerging at about the same period. Althusser, having assimilated and adapted some of Gramsci's ideas about hegemony and the distinction between political and civil society that we considered earlier, was attempting to theorize about the subtle mechanisms of control, at work in advanced capitalist societies, that enabled the maintenance of a particular social order, a particular set of relations of production and a particular exercise of power without that power being felt. Althusser believed, quite rightly, that modern power is no longer forceful, omnipotent and excessive but rather that it is exercised by stealth. Instead of individuals being regimented and directed, or even manipulated, they are incorporated. Through his notions of the 'repressive' and the 'ideological state apparatuses' Althusser informs us of both the 'iron hand' and the 'velvet glove'. Concretely he is talking about the police and the armed forces as opposed to education, mass media and belief systems, analytically he is revealing that the modern state fails in its desire to rule by consent if the populace comes too much into contact with the hard edge of power. The state is seeking the agreement rather than the coercion of its polity. He develops the mediating concept of 'interpellation', that is the manner in which modern ideologies claim the individual. The dominant ideology operates not as an opaque and compelling wall of ideas that impacts upon the consciousness of the collective; rather it selects and individualizes and penetrates the subject, thus it invites us singularly into its complex, and once in we act as if freely choosing the typical motives provided. The advertisement which 'advises' that to own a particular make of car is to display your obvious sexual prowess is not intended for your neighbour; the headteacher's cry of 'that boy!' across the packed assembly hall renders every pupil vulnerable to the status, and responsibility, of potential miscreant; and the billboard that exclaims 'Your Country Needs You' is certainly not speaking to the person standing behind you. Althusser's ideas concerning interpellation contributed to the burgeoning body of work on cultural reproduction by indicating the routine and systematic ways in which stasis is achieved within culture with the quasi-conscious compliance of the individual member of that culture.

Bourdieu had developed and expanded his central concepts of 'cultural capital' and 'habitus', which we shall consider in more detail later, and subsequently his own work and his influence upon the research of others spread into an examination of areas of concern beyond education, such as socialization, high culture and artistic practice, and style and mannerism in social relations.

Bourdieu's ideas and his method of analysis are both highly original, but also enlighteningly synthetic, in the good sense, of deriving through a cocktail of intellectual antecedents. Viewed in terms of the history of ideas, it is both interesting and important to note that despite the complex of traditions and influences which contribute to Bourdieu's thought the British tradition of the sociology of culture and cultural studies seems to have picked up on and crystallized around the largely negative and critical elements of his thesis. Ensuing from this a majority of contributions to this field have developed the metaphor of reproduction as copy or imitation rather than as regeneration or synthesis. As a consequence 'cultural reproduction' has become subsumed under the orthodoxy of studies in the theory of ideology and neo-Marxisms.[3] Certain other different and significant bodies of work continued to develop the positive side, such as Bernstein's[4] extended studies of the role of socio-linguistic codes in revealing the character of the relation between the social structure and the symbolic order, and also Cicourel's[5] research into cognitive sociology which revolved around the acquisition of interpretive procedures. In spite of these important initiatives, and others, the central concept of cultural reproduction had, however, become seemingly hijacked within a deep structural conspiracy of overde-termination which almost precluded redemption.

It is of course important, and for some theorists wholly proper, to address the well-established theme of ideology and structural determinacy in cultural reproduction theory; however there are other available approaches. Part of what this chapter will recommend is a series of attempts to open up other possibilities from a variety of perspectives less familiar in this area of study like, for example, reflexive sociology, Durkheimian sociology, ethnomethodology, structuralism and post-structuralism. Cultural reproduction is also an important and challenging theme in any discussion of postmodernism, with its emphasis on simulacra, representation and cultural production.

It will be useful, at this stage, to examine the place of the concepts of culture and thus cultural reproduction within social theory more generally. All sociological explanations begin with some concept of *structure* which, following Durkheim,[6] appears as typical to all societal members; that is, it stands as the normal, the mundane, it has a series of taken-for-granted manifestations. Structure is also constraining upon the conduct of members either overtly or, more successfully, through a network of covert strategies. Finally, structure is to be recognized as ultimately independent of the will or caprice of particular individuals. It is then a determinate form, intangible but real, and always real in its consequences. Structure provides the supra-individual source of causality in sociological reasoning whether it is experienced by members, or constituted by theorists, as economic, political, moral, cognitive or even physical in its orientation. From these various conceptions, or, perhaps we should say, formulations, stem the dynamics in social theory that we might call *process*. Culture and particularly cultural reproduction are precisely dynamics that we would gather within this notion of process. Indeed, the idea of culture emerges from the noun 'process', in the sense of nurture, growth and bringing into being – in fact, to cultivate in an agricultural or horticultural sense.[7] Culture, as process, is emergent, it is forthcoming, it is continuous in the way of re-producing and, as with all social processes, it provides the grounds for and the parallel context of *social action* itself.

All social action, within sociology, appears not in isolation but rather depends upon its context or a sense of competence for its meaning. In this way it stands as an index of the social occasion from which it arose.[8] Action therefore inevitably relates back to the original, but perhaps unspoken, social structure for its coherence and intelligibility. The point of this excursion into the patterning of sociological explanation is twofold: firstly, that sociology has a perpetually ambivalent relationship with the centrality and efficacy of subjectivity, selves become movements

within culture or parts of cultural units, and secondly, that sociology appears to generate one sense of a causal chain but what
we have essentially is a teleology, a circuit of explanation that is
self-sustaining in terms of the object of its completion; as
Durkheim put it, 'explain the social in terms of the social'.

An important analytic point here, particularly in the study of
a symbolic structure like culture, is that the patterning of these
modalities *structure, process* and *social action* is not descriptive,
although in some epistemological guises, like, for example, positivism, it passes itself off as if it were wholly descriptive. However, and this is a point worthy of emphasis, this patterning of
modalities is not descriptive: rather it is metaphoric. The metaphors become our analytic topic. Those cultural signs or conventions, as metaphors, become our topic. Our choice of metaphors
and our choice through cultural metaphors expresses our
interests, our intentions and our moral relation to the world. The
use of different metaphors in our analysis displays our attitude
to a knowledge of the social world and its cultures; it reveals our
vision and that also of our tradition. For example, it is, or should
be by now, commonplace to attend critically to the invocation of
the masculine form 'Man' to summon up images of all humankind in western reason or indeed in much public discourse, hence
the new use of 'chairperson'. At a more esoteric level it is perhaps
less routine to acknowledge the empiricist legacy of the centrality
of the senses, particularly vision, in much social theory that 'looks
at', 'sees' and specifically 'observes' its phenomena; this has even
permeated everyday speech where we enquire 'do you see what
I mean?' We may note further the technical and commercial
metaphoricity that has permeated much contemporary sociology;
for example, the invocation of terms like 'production', 'profit',
'output'; even in the often bureaucratic prose of such theorists
as Habermas[9] when he is, ironically, levelling a critique at the
penetration of the discourse of science and technology into the
life-world, thus militating against a free democracy.

The point, I trust, should be clear. Different metaphors
unconsciously or, in the case of reflexive theorizing, consciously
display our varieties of moral commitment and thus our different
perspectives on social life. In this gathering of ideas, in this
process of signification, our central metaphors are 'culture' and
'reproduction' and we should now examine these metaphors in
order to liberate their potential meanings.

Thus far we have introduced the concept of culture in relation to the ideas of process and growth, and extracted a view that culture carries with it a sense of becoming. Earlier, in Chapter 2, we also looked at the relationship between culture and social structure. We can rehearse some of these arguments here but we also need to know what is culture as distinct from society, or do the terms duplicate? Malinowski[10] tells us that culture is '. . . inherited artefacts, goods, technical process, ideas, habits and values'. Included within his definition is a notion of social structure which, he believed, could not be understood apart from culture. He further states that culture 'obviously is the integral whole consisting of the implements and consumer goods, of constitutional charters for the various social groupings, of human ideas and crafts, beliefs and customs' and he continues that 'the essential fact of culture as we live it and experience it, as we observe it scientifically, is the organisation of human beings into permanent groups'.

Firth,[11] another eminent anthropologist, adopts a different position and distinguishes firmly between social structure and culture, defining the latter as 'the component of accumulated resources, immaterial as well as material, which a people inherit, employ, transmute, add to and transmit; it is all learned behaviour which has been socially acquired'.

Bottomore[12] writing as a sociologist, concludes my inventory of definitions with the proposition that: 'By culture we mean the ideational aspects or social life, as distinct from the actual relations and forms of relationship between individuals; and by *a* culture the ideational aspects of *a* particular society.'

It would appear that the concept of culture implies a relationship with the accumulated shared symbols representative of and significant within a particular community, what we might describe as a context-dependent semiotic system. Culture, however, is not simply a residue, it is, as we have already considered, in progress; it processes and reveals as it structures and contains. Culture is the way of life and the manner of living of a people. It is often conflated with the idea of high culture; this is an understanding both too restrictive and too exclusive, yet high culture is our topic also; and this binary definition has been a constant theme throughout this book in terms of exclusion, compatibility and also confusion.

Let us now explore our second root metaphor, that of 'reproduction'. A phenotypical reading of the term, or what I have previously referred to as a 'negative' definition, invokes all of the modern and sterile resonances of mechanicism and technicism, it speaks of a crafted or rather fashioned re-production. At its strongest we have a copy or repeat, at its most dilute an imitation or a likeness; within this limited sense of the term we are presented with reproduction as replication; this is a metaphor of constraint. In relation to the experience of social life, such reproduction must be an affirmation of the ancien régime, a system which extols a symbolic violence through its containment of choice in the present.[13] The symbolism of such an order is condensed, opaque and referential of convention, form and demise.

Alternatively, a genotypical reading of reproduction is, in juxtaposition, positive and vibrant. It brings to mind the excitement and newness of sexual and biological reproduction. Here the image is generative rather than replicative and it offers the possibilities of change and new combinations. The very idea of birth that stems from such a formulation is innovative and necessarily creative. Here is the theorizing of the new or coming order and the social is conceived of through change, re-formation or even revolution. The symbolism is diffuse and elusive, it lives within rules-in-use as meaning. Both of these understandings of our concept culture, which are well rehearsed by Williams,[14] can be taken to relate to other pervasive binary combinations in social theory, such as continuity and change, consensus and conflict, structure and agency, and determinism and free will. The fluidity that exists in the space between these oppositions is itself infinitely reproductive and generative of varieties of theorizing. It is also this territory left vacant amidst the avenues of post-Enlightenment dichotomies that is being colonized by the polysemy of postmodern critique, that we shall discuss in the next chapter.

CULTURAL REPRODUCTION: THE MARXIST PERSPECTIVE

The theme of cultural reproduction is one that has arisen from within a diversity of forms of contemporary social investigation, all of which variously but inevitably refer to a sense of social continuity achieved through modalities of change. Now in one dominant form this appears as a classical Marxist dichotomy between *essence* (continuity) and *appearance* (as change) and indeed, as previously suggested, much of the British work on cultural reproduction emerges from a Marxist tradition, but by no means all. It is important, I would suggest, to attempt to liberate the concept back into the wider arena of sociological debate. But, to begin with, let us look briefly at the constitution of a Marxist method in terms of essence and appearance. This is an epistemology initiated in *The German Ideology,* refined in *The Introduction to the Critique of Political Economy* and the *Grundrisse* and one reaching its fruition in *Das Kapital.* The classical examples of this method derive from Volume 1 of this last source, *Das Kapital.* In my chapter on Culture and Materialism (Chapter 4) we looked at the instance of 'commodity fetishism'; here we shall take our example from the section on 'Wages'. Wages, Marx argues, produce a distorted and distorting image of the relationship between people in the market place. One group, the owners of the means of production, appear to offer wages to the working group in return for the exercise of their labour. Labour then is treated as if it were like any other commodity, it is assumed to be objective and it can be assigned an exchange value. Labour, however, is unlike any other commodity; it is, in reality, subjective, it is part of our species being *homo laborens.* The consumption of labour generates a value in excess of its original unmobilized state. This peculiar property of labour is called 'labour power'.

Despite the *appearance* of wages as providing a fair exchange for the consumption of labour, what is actually being appropriated is 'labour power', it is generating a 'surplus value' or a profit for its consumer. The *essence* of the wages relation is, then, the true relation of 'exploitation', and whatever changes might occur in the appearance of wages (trade union bargaining, wage increases, improved conditions of service) the mechanism of exploitation, as the essence, is always reproduced. So in Marx's terms we have an elementary example of how components of a market culture are reproduced such that the real relations that benefit the old order remain intact and hidden. The linking concept for this contradiction or discrepancy between appearance and essence is, of course, ideology. Ideology becomes the process, both conscious but largely unconscious, through which a distortion, blurring, generalizing and decontextualizing of realities occurs; all to the benefit of one particular group within the society. We are provided, through this model, with a pattern and a battery of concepts for the analysis of any cultural phenomenon extending from the material forms like property, artefacts or commodities (things-in-themselves), to the ideational like language, knowledge and subjectivity itself. Indeed Althusser's concept of 'interpellation' offered precisely the possibility of identity and subjectivity emerging from the ideological process. Ideology being a constant variable in social life, it hails and elects individuals, it incorporates them and provides them with purpose and a sense of self. The determinacy of distortion is complete, the realm of the private is invaded and inhabited by the grinding inevitability of ideological necessity. History teaches us odd lessons and although, as we have become even more poignantly aware due to recent events in Eastern Europe, Marxism as a concrete economic and political policy has generated a series of social structures which manifest oppression and, at the personal level, despair, in the context of western theorizing the tradition has always provided for the possibility of freedom, emancipation and authenticity as intellectual principles. Nevertheless, in the context of cultural analysis in terms of culture's re-producibility, work emanating from such a theoretical perspective provides a vision of pessimism, of regret and of fallenness, Adorno's 'melancholy science'. Thus its often unspoken recommendations provide the grounds for upheaval and conflict, a thesis of constant redemption. As a form of analysis Marxist theory espouses a democracy which is, however, overseen and directed by the hidden expert, the defiler of reified images and the revealer of distortions.

CULTURAL REPRODUCTION: THE DURKHEIMIAN PERSPECTIVE

Durkheimian sociology provides another, relatively under-exercised, resource for cultural reproduction theory. This tradition centres on an unashamed expert who wishes to 'speak louder than commonsense'; indeed at an early stage of *The Rules of Sociological Method* Durkheim tells us that we must 'eradicate all preconceptions', which Hirst[15] has interpreted as an assault on the ideology of common sense. Durkheim is certainly making a claim for the establishment of a form of discourse that is disciplined, unconventional and reflexive upon the commonplace. He directs us to proceed from the local and the particular experience of everyday life, the individual manifestation, to the real, the typical, the collective representation. From an understanding of this realm of phenomena we can generate an altruistic commitment to the development of a truly moral science. Morality, in Durkheim, refers to that which binds people together, the essential adhesion or bond which must reproduce from moment to moment in order to sustain any experience of cohesion or indeed sociality itself.

The problem, for Durkheim, with the issues of social and cultural reproduction is not to reveal their occurrence behind the distorted ideological mask of change but rather to search for the appropriate collective secular credo that will 'ensure' reproduction of solidarity in the face of change. Reproduction is not taken to be intrinsically evil, or even necessarily partial in its implications. Durkheim offers us this thesis, which is fundamental to all of his writings,[16] in *The Division of Labour*. It is in this formative work that he provides the two pervasive models of integration across the axis of modernity in the form of 'mechanical' and 'organic' solidarity. Mechanical solidarity is a societal form based on sameness, on compact, shared beliefs, on an ill-defined division of labour and on an intensely other-directed collective consciousness. The transition to organic solidarity, which occurs through 'moral density' accompanying the passage of modernity, brings about a steady and debilitating enfeeblement of this collective consciousness which has a knock-on effect on the other features of the society. The division of labour becomes clearly demarcated and rigorously policed, belief systems diffuse and dissemble, and the point of recognition between people becomes utter difference. The change might be summarized, within a science of ethics, as a movement away from altruism into the ascendance of egoism. Durkheim's purpose, and his legacy, is to produce a theory of benign reproduction. A theory that will locate the binding force in the face of potential fragmentation; what he described as the condition of 'anomie'. His work is reparative and displays a vigorous impulse to reconstruct difference as interdependence. In opposition to the Marxist approach Durkheim is informing us of the very necessity of cultural reproduction, the necessity of conformity through change. Some systems simply must reproduce; his societal forms are, after all, not evolutionary but morphological. The Durkheimian tradition views reproduction with an optimism, indeed a positivism; its metaphors are consensual rather than divisive and its motivation is integrative.

CULTURAL REPRODUCTION: THE
ETHNOMETHODOLOGICAL PERSPECTIVE

A further source of the genre of cultural reproduction theory, namely ethnomethodology, may be seen instructively in the wake of the Durkheimian tradition. Garfinkel,[17] the Californian pioneer of ethnomethodology, though notably influenced by Schutzian phenomenology, in terms of the socially constructed yet typical character of reality; Parsonian systems theory, through the unquestionable centrality of the problem of order, albeit reconstituted as an internal rather than an external issue; and Wittgenstein's linguistic philosophy in relation to language games and rules-in-use, is also very much in debt to Durkheim. Durkheim's realization of a 'collective consciousness' is instructive of Garfinkel's sense of the taken-for-grantedness of social members' everyday knowledge. This is apparent throughout his work but, perhaps, most explicit in Garfinkel's early paper 'Conditions for successful degradation ceremonies'.[18] Ethnomethodology relies upon a strong sense of a collective but inarticulate consensus in its explanations of human conduct which it describes ironically, in the context of its contest with positivist rhetoric, as the 'normal'. This normal implies not the normative against which we can judge the deviant or pathological but rather the routine, the taken-for-granted, that which we all must know in order to assume the status of a member in everyday culture. Cultural reproduction, for ethnomethodologists, is almost a necessary process, indeed it is a purpose. The artful practices of members that ethnomethodology reveals and celebrates for us in the intricate ethnographic detail or, most usually, conversational exchange, is dedicated, though not determined, to make sense of its context by reflexively reproducing the conditions of its own occurrence. Thus reproduction for members is both intentional and integrative. It is a constant reaffirmation of collective life. A major departure by ethnomethodology, in relation to the sociological tradition, is the dissolution of the role of theorist as expert. It asserts that the sociologist, in accounting for the character of social life, is exercising the same skills and practices as the lay member; it is simply that the sociologist is reflexive back upon these practices. Whatever the status of this utopian democratic claim on behalf of this body of work it reiterates the necessary role of both theorist and lay member as agents in the reproduction of a continuous and shared symbolic network that we can call culture.

CULTURAL REPRODUCTION: THE STRUCTURALIST PERSPECTIVE

Structuralism provides our final, but compelling, input to cultural reproduction theory. This is no uniformity of approach but an internally divisive spectrum of attitudes towards human affairs that shares certain common themes. Structuralism contains and combines many elements of the previously mentioned approaches but reworks the classical epistemological dichotomy between *essence* and *appearance* in terms of the continuum between *depth* and *surface*. It was Lévi-Strauss[19] who was primarily instrumental in exercising this geological metaphor. He likens the formation of cultural phenomena to the layering, expanding, contracting and intruding of rock strata; each configuration of topography appearing unique but sharing certain underlying elements with similar geological phenomena. The understanding of such phenomena is to be conducted through the excavation of these strata and a subsequent exposure of their patterns of inter-relation. The structure derives from the pattern. Elements of a culture, as we experience them, are the surface appearances or manifestations of underlying patterns at a deeper level, both within time, the 'synchronic', and through time, the 'diachronic'. Ferdinand de Saussure,[20] the Swiss linguist, originally provided, through his science of signs, what now stands as perhaps the most significant and binding element of all structuralisms; it is that the underlying patterns or structure of any cultural phenomenon is to be understood in terms of a linguistic metaphor. We may come to know the structures that comprise a culture as if they were a language. The lexical terms or items of vocabulary within such a language are provided for by the symbols that exist within social life, that is, the representations that attach to or arise from the tangible state of things or materiality itself; for example, kinship roles such as mother, son, cousin, grandfather and so on. The grammatical rules of this metaphoric language are provided for by the act, the continuous and habitual act, of signification; which would be the permissable relationships between kin, and the taboos that attach to their transgression. So the variety of ways that we make sense in different cultures variously articulates and therefore gives rise to the different 'languages' that our cultural symbols comprise. The complexity of this system of meaning is compounded by the essentially arbitrary relation between any particular object or state of affairs and the symbolic (linguistic) device that is employed to signify its being. Thing-like-ness then, as objective and recognizable within any culture derives not from any correspondence between name and named but from a delicately poised structuring of otherness in our contained network of ideas. Things are not so much what they are but emerge from a knowledge of what they are not, in fact from a system of oppositions, the principle at the core of any binary code. Now the fragility of this structuring of otherness remains unthreatened, indeed it appears as robust through the very practice of sociality, through the persistence and reproduction of that tenuous relation at each and every turn within a culture. Meaning then, within a particular culture, emerges from convention overcoming the arbitrary relation between the signifier and the signified. Convention reproduces culture and culture is contingent upon reproduction within structuralism. Culture is a conventional, yet deep structural practice, the rules of which may be only part of the unconscious of its members. Cultural symbols and representations are the surface structure.

BOURDIEU AND CULTURAL REPRODUCTION

We can return now to the work of Bourdieu, the founder of our concept 'cultural reproduction', and we find elements of each of the major traditions considered above emergent in his writing and integrated seemingly without conflict or ambiguity.

It is apparent that Bourdieu is committed to the development of a critical yet appreciative theory of culture and as such his ideas provide an important contribution to our understanding of both power and authority within our society. He began from an analysis of the education system and the part that its institutions play in the constitution and transmission of what counts as legitimate knowledge and forms of communication.

> . . . the cultural field is transformed by successive restructurations rather then by radical revolutions, with certain themes being brought to the fore while others are set to one side without being completely eliminated, so that continuity of communication between intellectual generations remains possible. In all cases, however, the pat-

terns informing the thought of a given period can be fully
understood only by reference to the school system, which
is alone capable of establishing them and developing
them, through practice, as the habits of thought common
to a whole generation.[21]

In this sense Bourdieu is forging a positive link between the
symbolic order and the state of the social structure. He is demonstrating how forms and patterns of communication both reflect
and perpetuate particular communities. In this way his work has
much in common with Bernstein's theory of socio-linguistic codes
and both serve to blur the distinction between cultural reproduction and social reproduction. Bourdieu here reveals elements
of a Durkheimian epistemology through his interest in the sustaining character of cultural representations; through the production
and maintenance of a social consensus, a concept parallel in
importance to the idea of a 'collective consciousness'; and
through the assumption of the social origins and persistence of
knowledge classifications. He is, however, critical of what he sees
as Durkheim's positivism in that it depends upon stasis, and also
that Durkheim considers the functions of the education system
to be anticipated.[22]

Addressing the context of education Bourdieu conceptualizes
all pedagogic practice as, at one level, a style of inculcation that
perpetuates a more general social tendency towards repression,
what he refers to as a symbolic violence. Repression, within
Bourdieu's thesis, becomes a 'natural' mode of human adaptation
towards a culture that is pervasively oppressive. All forms of
socialization and enculturation are seen to contribute to this alienating adaptation. Here we see his obvious continuity with the
tradition of Marxism, its concerns with the corruption of social
structures through history and their visual refinement through
ideology. Bourdieu bears witness to a society based on constraint,
not a just or equitable constraint, but one organized in terms of
the unequal distribution of power in relation to the economic
order. He looks towards the sets of interests that ground particular social groupings and the selections of what constitute the
culturally located sense of reality for their members. He is critical
of the structures and institutions that engender, embody and
project images of 'what is the case' and he wishes to look beyond
and reveal the true conditions hidden by these mechanisms of
distortion.

The essential structuralism in Bourdieu's work is apparent throughout. He regards society as a surface structure of illusions from which, it is intended, his analysis will reveal the actual set of relations existing at the deep structural level. The transition between the levels will uncover homologies between previously disparate elements of the cultural system but simultaneously the individual actor will recede as a source of agency and intentionality in the construction of history.

Bourdieu has provided a major contribution to contemporary studies through his development of a series of forceful metaphors to articulate the subtle relation of the power and domination at work in the social world and through the stratification of culture. Most notable is that which he draws from political economy when he speaks of 'cultural capital': 'there is, diffused within a social space a cultural capital, transmitted by inheritance and invested in order to be cultivated'.[23]

Differential, and stratified, socialization practices, in combination with the system of education, function to discriminate positively in favour of those members of society who by virtue of their location within the class system are the 'natural' inheritors of cultural capital. This is no crude conspiracy theory of a conscious manipulation. Rather what is being explored here is the possibility of a cultural process that is self-sustaining and self-perpetuating. This process is regarded as carrying with it a context of anticipation and tolerance of stratification and privilege. In this way Bourdieu moves from the ideological function of culture into an awareness of the peculiar efficacy of culture in that it is seen as structuring the system of social relations by its functioning. Apprehended in the context of Bourdieu's analysis the education system thus comes to be treated as the means by which social privilege is allocated and confirmed and it is the myth of pedagogic practice as being value free that enables this process to complete. This myth is all-engrossing in its opacity, that is, it envelops all groups within society and thus produces complementary versions of the 'natural' order. Neither dominant nor oppressed groups suspect this latent function of the educational system and consequently perfect integrity is maintained at the level of each individual consciousness. 'School serves to transform the collective heritage into the common individual unconscious.'[24]

Following from this, as Bourdieu makes clear, even within a democratic society this manifestation of a disguised machinery continues to re-establish the inequalities of a social order which is pre-democratic in character and anti-democratic in essence.

Included within Bourdieu's definition of culture are all semiotic systems, ranging from language as a communicative network, through science to art and literature; all instances of a symbolic universe. He argues that all societal members actively involved in the creation and expressive reconstruction of such systems do so against the assumed backdrop of freedom and neutrality. This he points to as a grand illusion that is disguising the true political function of culture. As all members assume and become aware of reality through and within culture, they inevitably and unknowingly have the structure of existing power relations thrust upon them. This is a clear instance of what Bourdieu refers to as symbolic violence. The particular status groups who confer cultural legitimacy, like teachers and critics, conduct their professional roles and distribute merit with reference to an absolute index of intrinsic worth. This index and its acceptance mystifies the actual political situation, that cultural judgements and ranking are grounded in the protection of particular interests – indices of worth speak not of an absolute but of power and domination. The area of creative and artistic freedom is accounted for by Bourdieu through linking its emergence with the historical development and automization of the system of production and consumption of cultural goods. This historical process generates what Bourdieu refers to as an *intellectual field*. Young[25] clearly summarizes this concept as follows:

He [Bourdieu] conceives of the 'intellectual field' as the mediating set of agencies in which various groups of producers compete for cultural legitimacy. In elaborating on the idea of 'intellectual field' Bourdieu suggests the social and economic context for three aspects of the literary and art 'worlds' that are normally taken for granted. 1) The belief in 'art for art's sake'. 2) The assumption of the public's incompetence and the consequent refusal of artists to respond to public demands. 3) The growth of a group of critics who interpret artistic work for the public and give it legitimacy. Bourdieu refers to the 'creative project' as the activity in which the demands of the 'intellectual field' and the external context of the social and economic order of the time are joined in the work of art itself. Thus he suggests works of art and

literature are formed in the context of public categories
of definitions like 'nouvelle vague' and 'new novel' in
terms of which the artist is defined and defines himself.[26]

One more important concept in Bourdieu's work is that of the
habitus. This idea provides a link between the structuring of
social relationships and the culture of a society. The habitus
constitutes 'the principle that regulates the act', it is typified as
'the system of modes of perception, of thinking, of appreciation
and of action'.[27] The habitus is a concept that seems to take
meaning at a number of different levels: it is in one sense the
metaphor for membership of a community grounded in intellectual or aesthetic considerations yet it is also available as a key to
integration into a Durkheimian creed of solidarity, a key that is
acquired in early socialization. So, for example, if we treat language as a habitus, it can be seen that certain ways of speech
provide for membership of particular communities. These forms
of speech, which instance membership, are far more than mere
media for communication; they speak more than they can say.
Such forms of speech are totemic, they are emblems, they symbolize the particular group, they carry with them the group's
particular interests and orientations, and they display the group's
thought style. At its most concrete, and yet still remarkably
subtle, a sense of habitus may be rendered as 'style'. This is an
idea foreign to most British social analysts (even after Hebdige)[28]
yet one absolutely central to the deep and painful recognition of
class variations through accents, knots in ties, ways of holding
cutlery and recognizing appropriate wine glasses, and so on.

Certain habitus, not unlike Bernstein's[29] restricted code,
stand in disjunction with the habitus of the dominant group; the
latter being the vehicle for a self-structuring sense of 'good taste',
'appropriate style', 'expressiveness' etc. all of which are deemed
meretricious within the institutions of the intellectual field. The
possessors of the dominant group habitus are the inheritors of
cultural capital; their forms of reality and cognition are always
appropriate ('you can always tell a gentleman . . .'). So different
habitus constitute different forms of programming or equipping
the individual such that he naturally gravitates towards his
eventual, and proper, location in the social hierarchy ('class will
out . . .').

It may be assumed that every individual owes to the
type of schooling he has received a set of basic, deeply

interiorised master-patterns on the basis of which he subsequently acquires other patterns, so that the system of patterns by which his thought is organised owes its specific character not only to the nature of the patterns constituting it but also to the frequency with which these are used and to the level of consciousness at which they operate, these properties being probably connected with the circumstances in which the most fundamental intellectual patterns were acquired.[30]

The primary function of education and different socialization variants is to transmit cultural capital in the form of particular valued signs and the styles of their presentation. Other habitus are consequently relegated to the status of stigma. Commonsense representations come to realize different social locatedness through differential talent, or even 'blood'. School failure and indeed social stratification is rendered 'naturally' intelligible and the political differentiating function of the education system and family structure is obscured through the fog of public consensus. Bourdieu's other major concept of the *cultural unconscious* resonates strongly with the notion of habitus and also the Durkheimian 'collective consciousness'. It is intangible and made real through external referents. It refers to the tacit, assumed and unspoken grounds which precondition any cultural production. Within Bourdieu's model the cultural unconscious has an elective affinity with the dominant social interests of the epoch.

NOTES

[1] See C. Jenks, *Cultural Reproduction*, London: Routledge (1993).

[2] L. Althusser, 'Ideological and repressive state apparatuses', in *Lenin and Philosophy and Other Essays*, London: New Left Books (1971).

[3] See M. Barrett, P. Corrigan, A. Kuhn and J. Wolff, *Ideology and Cultural Production*, Beckenham: Croom Helm (1979); T. Bennett, G. Martin, C. Mercer and J. Woollacott, *Culture, Ideology and Social Process*, London: Open University/Batsford (1981); M. Apple, *Cultural and Economic Reproduction in Education*, London: Routledge & Kegan Paul (1982).

[4] B. Bernstein, *Class, Codes and Control* Vols I, II & III, London: Routledge & Kegan Paul (1971–3).

[5] A. Cicourel, *Cognitive Sociology*, Harmondsworth: Penguin (1973).

[6] E. Durkheim, *The Rules of Sociological Method*, New York: Free Press (1938).

[7] R. Williams, *Keywords*, London: Fontana (1976).

[8] H. Garfinkel, *Studies in Ethnomethodology*, Englewood Cliffs, NJ: Prentice-Hall (1967).

[9] J. Habermas, *Toward a Rational Society*, London: Heinemann Educational Books (1971).

[10] B. Malinowski, *A Scientific Theory of Culture*, North Carolina: Chapel Hill (1944).

[11] R. Firth, *Elements of Social Organisation*, London: Tavistock (1971).

[12] T. Bottomore, *Sociology*, London: Allen and Unwin (1962).

[13] P. Bourdieu, 'Symbolic power' (trans C. Wringe), in D. Gleeson (ed.), *Identity and Structure*, Humberside, Driffield: Nafferton (1977).

[14] R. Williams, *Culture*, London: Fontana (1971).

[15] P. Hirst, *Durkheim, Bernard and Epistemology*, London: Routledge & Kegan Paul (1975).

[16] J. Smith and C. Jenks, *Durkheim, Art and Representation* (forthcoming).

[17] H. Garfinkel, *Studies in Ethnomethodology*, Englewood Cliffs, NJ: Prentice-Hall (1967).

[18] H. Garfinkel, 'Conditions for successful degradation ceremonies', *American Journal of Sociology* 61, March 1956, pp. 420–4.

[19] C. Lévi-Strauss, *Triste Topique*, London: Atheneum (1964).

[20] F. de Saussure, *Course in General Linguistics*, London: Peter Owen (1960).

[21] P. Bourdieu, 'Systems of education and systems of thought', in M. F. D. Young (ed.), *Knowledge and Control*, London: Collier-Macmillan (1971), p. 192.

[22] J. Kennett, 'The Sociology of Pierre Bourdieu', *Educational Review* Vol. 25, 1973.

[23] P. Bourdieu, op.cit., 'Systems of education', p. 201.

[24] Ibid., p. 200.

[25] M. F. D. Young, op. cit., pp. 10–11.

[26] P. Bourdieu, 'Intellectual field and creative project', in M. F. D. Young, op. cit.

[27] P. Bourdieu, 'Systems ⬛⬛⬛ on', op. cit.
[28] D. Hebdige, *Subcul⬛⬛ Meaning of Style*, London: Methuen (1979).
[29] B. Bernstein, *Cla⬛ and Control* Vols I, II and III, London: Routle⬛ ⬛an Paul (1971–3).
[30] P. Bourdieu, 'Sys⬛ education', op. cit.

7

Culture and postmodernism

Over the space of perhaps one decade, postmodernism has grown from the status of a mood to that of a reality; or at least a reality-in-thought. Its nebulous empire, projected forward by the tenuous and neurotic principles of self de-centring, the unrecognizability of priority and committed instability, has expanded in step with this elevation in status. What was once a localized, and healthy, concern with the limits of the modernist trajectory in fine art and architecture has grown beyond arrogance into hubris, and mounted a critique of modern life and, more particularly, of the forms of knowledge and value that support and sustain such living.

Postmodernism knows no discipline – though its protagonists write mostly from 'respectable' positions within traditions of thought; rather it envelopes as a corrosive sea mist and takes recognizable form either as an external attack on the methods and values of our time, or, simultaneously, as a spontaneous, intentional and internally generated symptom of our time. A phenomenon of this magnitude and scope is worthy of our concern; it affects our conceptions of culture, it challenges and perhaps changes our conceptions of culture, it may even, if some of its self-generated claims are to be internalized, constitute our culture.

Postmodernism does not proffer alternative ways of knowing from whence we might appropriately confront and appreciate the 'new', but instead it insinuates into all discourse, through a continuous scything at the knees of existing epistemologies, a sustained reduction and depotentiation of explanations that is premised upon the wholly unpriviledged quality of all discourses. Deriving from the deconstruction of post-structuralism Baudrillard has occupied the wasteland between the signifier and the signified and justified it in the manner of a diagnosis, and even celebration, of the entropic tendencies of our time. For Lyotard the difference between moral and political positions is as significant as the play of language games, and the theorist, the self, derives from the intersection and interface between these games – the *differend* – the synapses through which the various messages flow. The battle for the sign is clearly begun, without justification for any prior claims. The rule is that the rules do not stand. Within this swathe social theory stands or falls[1] as does the concept of culture itself.

Although the idea of postmodernism appears wilfully to elude definition, there being no discourse that could capture its project (there being no project), a courageous summation of its scattered parts is attempted by Hebdige, now an acclaimed high priest himself; he has the authority (ironically, there being no such privilege) to provide the necessary conceptual bin-liner.

> Postmodernism – we are told – is neither a homogeneous entity nor a consciously directed 'movement'. It is instead a space, a 'condition', a 'predicament', an *aporia*, an 'unpassable path' – where competing intentions, definitions, and effects, diverse social and intellectual tendencies and lines of force converge and clash. When it becomes possible for people to describe as 'postmodern' the decor of a room, the design of a building, the diagesis of a film, the construction of a record, or a scratch video, a television commercial, or an arts documentary, or the intertextual relations between them, the layout of a page in a fashion magazine or critical journal, an anti-teleological tendency within epistemology, the attack on the metaphysics of presence, a general attenuation of feeling, the collective chagrin and morbid projections of a post War

generation of baby boomers confronting disillusioned middle age, the predicament of 'reflexivity', a group of rhetorical tropes, a proliferation of surfaces, a new phase in commodity fetishism, a fascination for images, codes and styles, a process of cultural, political or existential fragmentation and/or crisis, the 'decentring' of the subject, an 'incredulity towards metanarratives', the replacement of unitary power axes by a plurality of power/discourse formations, the 'implosion of meaning', the collapse of cultural hierarchies, the dread engendered by the threat of nuclear self-destruction, the decline of the University, the functioning and effects of the new miniaturised technologies, broad societal and economic shifts into a 'media', 'consumer', or 'multinational' phase, a sense (depending on who you read) of placelessness (Jameson on the Bonnaventura Hotel) or the abandonment of placelessness (e.g. Kenneth Frampton's 'critical regionalism') or (even) a generalised substitution of spatial for temporal coordinates – when it becomes possible to describe all these things as 'postmodern' (or more simply using a current abbreviation, as 'post' or 'very post') then it's clear that we are in the presence of a buzzword.[2]

So there it is . . . an analytic scatterbomb waiting to be randomly secreted in argument by the cultural terrorist. The story behind postmodernism, although it resists the narrative form, is about the end of another and greater story. The concluding tale is that which was written by the Enlightenment. The Enlightenment established a set of typical characters, with typical motives and a shared goal, that is to say it provided the 'grand' narrative form for the history of modernity. Reason was to triumph over faith, humankind was to become the measure of all things, nature was to be quelled and put to the service of humankind, and time was to be measured in terms of a transition from darkness into the light, a transition and an implicit theory of moral evolution that came to be known as *progress*. The centrality of humankind and, following Descartes, cognitive subjectivism, when linked to the institutionalized mode of reason that we call science, was the methodology of this master plan. However, as history has shown us, the self-appointed claims of the methodology, those to objectivity, and the ideological insulation of its practitioners, in the form of value neutrality, have created an accelerative moral vacuum. World wars, techniques and technologies of mass extermination and a market-led programme of subsequently polluting productivity have all weighed in the deficit column to offset the gains in health, income, enlightenment, democratization and overall quality of life. Is this then the state of modernity that warrants the new designation – postmodernism? More than this surely? . . . or perhaps less.

NIETZSCHEAN INCEPTION

The prince of irrationalism, Nietzsche, the newly (re)discovered philosopher of the postmodern, had, it is argued, predicted and applauded the advent of this age of negative alchemy. His philosophical stylistics was, there is no doubt, concerned with morality – its redundancy and disassembly, to be more precise. Nietzsche made a series of sonorous pronouncements concerning the topic and purpose of philosophy and the weaknesses and degenerations that its conventional forms had wrought. Most serious and lasting is that uttered in the allegorical guise of *Zarathustra*, the pilgrim of postmodernity, descending from his ten years of contemplation on the mountain top, accompanied only by wisdom and pride, and witnessing the wastelands of humanity around him, 'God is dead' he declares, repeatedly. Now this is no simple sociological observation concerning the secularization of modern western society, although it may be superstructural to such a phenomenon. What the philosopher is announcing is the collapse of the centre and the consequent decentralization of value. In contradistinction to all of those turn-of-the-century metaphors from social theory stressing 'integration', 'solidarity', 'community', 'structure', 'instrumentality' and 'culture' itself, in sum, the language of *unification*, Nietzsche is recommending *dispersion*. The survival of the human spirit rests no longer in the hands of collectivities but in the affirmation of the new warrior, the individual in the incarnation of the *Ubermensch* (the overman). Humankind must escape from the protective politics of order into an affirmation of life as 'the will to power'. Herewith are the seeds of our new cultural critic.

> *I teach you the overman*. Man is something that shall be overcome. What have you done to overcome him? All beings so far have created something beyond themselves;

and do you want to be the ebb of this great flood and
even go back to the beasts rather than overcome man?
What is the ape to man? A laughingstock or a painful
embarrassment. And man shall be just that for the overman: a laughingstock or a painful embarrassment. You
have made your way from worm to man, and much in
you is still worm. . . .

Behold, I teach you the overman. The overman is
the meaning of the earth. Let your will say: the overman
shall be the meaning of the earth! I beseech you, my
brothers, *remain faithful to the earth*, and do not believe
those who speak to you of otherworldly hopes! Poison-
mixers are they, whether they know it or not. Despisers
of life are they, decaying and poisoned themselves, of
whom the earth is weary: so let them go.[3]

Nietszche is a didactic rather than a persuasive philosopher; he
is forthright in telling people how best to live their lives and the
key lies not in some collective ethic, either religious or secular,
but in the overthrowal of the beliefs and conventions of the
common person. *Zarathustra* espouses three significant doctrines
being: the will to power, the suspicion and revaluation of values,
and the eternal return. Life is not a rehearsal and does not benefit
from modesty, obedience or claiming second place. The will to
power is the existential self-affirmation of destiny through auth-
entic and reflexive choice. The values of others are obstacles to
the realization of the will, they are inhibiting and, particularly in
the form of collective beliefs like Christianity, are constraining
and worthy of violent opposition. Values, ideologically designated
as 'virtues', such as *pity* and *meekness*, are corrupting and depo-
tentiating of the will to power. It must be the *Ubermensch* who
will inherit the earth, but not in a finite state. This is no millennial
philosophy searching for the 'good' society in a stable recognizable form – such is the discourse of Marx, Weber and Durkheim,
the 'conventional' theorists – there is no *entelechy* for Nietzsche:
his *telos* is in the instability of process. The power of the will and
the constant revaluation of values are the 'good', in themselves.
No 'end' point can, or should, be envisaged, no new or improved
set of values is the purpose of being, but only the challenge of
convention. If there can be no end then the process built on the
'grand narrative', 'myth' or 'values' of history is nothing more

than an eternal return of circumstances, values, people and things.

Nietzsche's philosophical position is well summarized in the title of one of his last works *Beyond Good and Evil*, an amoral and apolitical locus from which to 'deconstruct' the thought and practice of other, more embodied and contexted, epistemologies and codes. His intuitive, anti-deductionist, anti-rationalist ideas challenge the classical tradition of philosophy and fly in the face of the metaphysical project, a knowledge of being. All metaphysical systems and ethical paradigms disguise assumptions and interests that are committed to the preservation of a weak stasis, the stagnation of the will and the triumph of mediocrity over the strength of creative being.

Following in the wake of this violent assault on the social ethic is the clamouring Babel that postmodernism designates 'polysemy', the many voices within a culture waiting to be heard all with an equivalence and a right, ranging from the oppressed to, simply, the previously unspoken.

POST-STRUCTURALIST GESTATION

The conduit for this vociferous Hydra is provided by the post-structuralist project, the era of 'difference'. The Nietzschean heritage turned left to emerge in the form of the French intellectual avant-garde through such writers as Derrida, Foucault, Donzelot, Deleuze and Guattari.

The theory of signs propounded by de Saussure had, through the amplification of Lévi-Strauss's structuralism, established the premise that all cultural phenomena are primarily linguistic in character. More than this, the cultural/linguistic system had come to be characterized, at a formal level, as an arbitrary but finite rule system capable of generating any number of other rule systems. The system has no biological necessity, and it is arbitrary also in terms of its symbols. The potential built into such a cultural system lay in its power in realizing an infinite range of realities. Relations between people could be reordered as a direct consequence of the formal properties of the cultural system. Thus the fact of human language, the fact of human culture, creates the potential for instability in the structure of communication. Meaning in culture, as in language, became a matter of 'difference'. Through the anti-conventionalist will to power, through a sustained 'deconstruction' of the values of the system, through a commitment to the 'instability of process' post-structuralism pressed this premise further.

> If structuralism divided the sign from the referent . . .
> 'post-structuralism' – goes a step further: it divides the signifier from the signified.
>
> Another way of putting what we have just said is that meaning is not immediately *present* in a sign. Since the meaning of a sign is a matter of what the sign is *not*, its meaning is always in some sense absent from it too. Meaning, if you like, is scattered or dispersed along the whole chain of signifiers: it cannot be easily nailed down, it is never fully present in any one sign alone, but is rather a kind of constant flickering of presence and absence together. Reading a text is more like tracing this process of constant flickering than it is like counting the beads on a necklace.[4]

Derrida's leading role in post-structuralism's revaluation of meaning, though widely adopted as a model in cultural analysis, has a distinctly 'text-centred' form. Indeed all other cultural phenomena may be regarded as of the same genre as text or metaphoric representations of text. The implications of his disassembly of reference in meaning and also of the status of the subject in knowing are serious for our formulations of an increasingly relativized and fluid sense of the 'cultural'. If meaning derives continuously from a play of signifiers, a reprise of the instability of process, and we begin perpetually from the belief that 'all the world's a text' then that which is known or knowable is beyond the province of mere subjectivity. Is it, perhaps, in search of a 'transcendental signifier' in the form of a universal consciousness? Indeed, the assault on the 'metaphysics of presence', previously refered to, is a strategy for breaking down the phenomenological grounding in intentionality which had grown out of the Cartesian centring of the *cogito*, the subject, the self. Through Derrida we can no longer depend on the necessity or reliability of the self-present and self-referential practices of understanding that have come to provide for the 'Reason' behind western, post-Enlightenment consciousness. The 'difference' established by de Saussure has become, for Derrida, insufficient to handle the problem of signification. He, therefore, introduces the new concept of *differance* which, though immensely complex, is succinctly defined by Callinicos:

> This neologism is what Lewis Carroll would have called a 'portmanteau word'. It combines the meanings of the two words 'to differ' and 'to defer'. It affirms, first, the priority of play and difference over presence and absence, and secondly, the necessity within difference of a relation to presence, a presence always deferred (into the future or past) but nevertheless constantly invoked. Presence is as intrinsic to difference as absence.[5]

There is no longer a closed system of meaning, but rather an open horizon to infinite possibilities and substitutions, with no certainty provided for the subject except through the falsehood of cultural convention. Reality is aestheticized and cultural forms are as but stylistic modes and devices within a written (but de-authored) text.

Beyond Derrida's 'textual' view of culture Foucault and his disciples have taken another way. Their post-structuralist socio-cultural theory has dispensed with, or 'deconstructed', the oppressive causality of structure. Thus, any account of action became an account of the interface between politics and psychology, which is what we see in Donzelot's analysis of the family as a unit of control, or Foucault's many analyses of the constitution of subjects (or person-hood) through penology, sexuality, insanity or medical regimes. Such work is providing a 'history of the present' through a series of imaginative genealogies of modernity. Nietzsche's will to power is revised as a 'will to truth' and the new synchronics of the past become realized as 'power-knowledge'.

Escaping from the anti-human poetics of Derrida's *Grammatology* we encounter a somewhat more embodied politic in Foucault's stories of timeless and yet infinitely connected instances of the exercise of power which make for the subject.

> For Foucault, it is the endless recursive spirals of power and knowledge: the total, timeless space he creates around the hellish figure of the panopticon: the viewing tower at the centre of the prison yard – the *voir* in savoir/pouvoir, the looking in knowing.[6]

Culture(s) for Foucault are not made up of lineage and heritage which may be understood under the name of tradition. Such a thesis on the continuity of collective understanding is both referential, with a priority to the signifier, and subject-based which atomizes knowledge through the concept of 'idea' and thus detracts from the larger purpose. This larger purpose is that of understanding history outside the 'classical episteme' and the totalizing fiction of the 'grand narrative'. Foucault's archaeologies of knowledge provide us with appraisals of 'discursive formations' which both escape the determinisms and reductionisms of historiography, and also enable the play of cultural signifiers to provide for meaning in contexts beyond the text. Here then the eternal recurrence of Nietzsche is appeased and the 'ontic'/'ontological' of Heidegger is presented in challenge to the completion of metaphysics through history.

The field of culture, within Foucault's vision, is constituted through a symbolic system which must be viewed with the utmost suspicion. The system, as a play of signifiers, is a construction of meaning through the exercise of power. The aesthetic may embody political rationality; relationality and even intimacy may operate through surveillance; and the mundane artefact or taken-for-granted formation carries with it synchronicities of control and inhibition in other areas of social life. Thus Foucault invokes the concept of 'governmentality' which is 'the ensemble formed by the institutions, procedures, analyses and reflections, the calculations and tactics, that allow the exercise of this very specific albeit complex form of power, which has as its target population'.[7]

Drawn, as one easily is, into the pleasurable tyranny of exotic post-structuralist prose, it is too easy to forget or deride its political input to the study of culture, most notably in the area of feminist analysis, and most eloquently through the work of Kristeva. Just as the Foucauldian school had dispensed with the concept of structure in the explanation of socio-cultural phenomena, so also had the feminist perspective begun to critique the 'totalizing' impulsions of such a notion. Although an important stage in the development of a gendered politic, first-wave feminism was still working with structural issues: the demand for equal rights that stemmed from liberal feminism, and the revelation of the exploitation and oppression accompanying the roles of domestic labour, the reserve army of labour and childcare, that Marxist feminism moved to centre stage. A second wave of theorizing was emerging which required the recognition of the centrality of 'sexuality' and 'gender' to identity and subjectivity. Post-structuralism, in its irreverent and will-to-power-full demolition of the finite boundaries of meaning, executed the destruction of the 'combinatories' or 'binary oppositions' that had been so central to de Saussure's language system and Lévi-Strauss's cultural system (which had discussed the 'exchange of women'). Most pervasive of these binaries, and most pertinent to the prevention or facilitation of a 'feminized' culture, were those of man/woman, culture/nature and the cognitive/affective.

POSTMODERNISM: THE FRUITION

Another significant, but often underplayed or forgotten, element in the mixing of the postmodern cocktail is the contribution of liberal and even conservative sociological theories concerning the altered structure of social relations in late modernity. Bell, proclaiming an end to ideology, arguably instigated the 'visible' era of the 'post- ' with his thesis describing the shift in both the mode and the relations of production. The productive base, Bell and also Touraine inform us, had shifted, through market forces and advances in technology, into the *post-industrial*, and the system of social stratification, long since recognizable in terms of polarization and now steadily thickening at the waist, had altered, such as to diffuse conventional class antagonisms into the *post-capitalist*. These two concepts, Bauman tells us, 'have served the purpose well: they sharpened our attention to what is new and discontinuous, and offered a reference point for counter arguments in favour of continuity'.[8] What has occurred beyond this, it may be suggested, is a conceptual drift, a crude assumption that postmoderism is, in some sense, the direct efflux of these potentially altered structural conditions: that it is a superstructural realization of shifts in the material base. This is an appropriation that one could ascribe to Lyotard when he states that postmodernism 'designates the state of our culture following the transformations which, since the end of the nineteenth century, have altered the game rules for science, literature and the arts'.[9]

This would appear to provide postmodernism with an objective status. It is now descriptive of 'the state of our culture', it is not reducible to being merely an idea, an abstraction, a mood or a fashion. Lyotard's manifesto is more than suggestive, it is legislative and covertly value laden. It sweeps away the triumphs of reason and political struggle throughout western history (an alternative set of values) and it opens the forum to the malcontentions of an infinity of factional interests which 'must now be heard'. Its values, if they may be designated as such, are those of disappointment, futility, despair and anarchy. It is as if 'anything goes' in the manner of a true nihilism. The tragedy of this injunction, as also recommended for scientific method by Feyerabend,[10] is that whereas some 'things' should be heard with a voice loud enough to silence common sense, *all* things 'go' with a competitive equivalence and are thus diffused under the banner of the postmodern. We are led into absurdities, such as Ellis treating the 'serial killer' as a metaphor for the truly postmodern man, or being asked by Baudrillard to imagine that the Gulf War only took place within our television sets. This is a high price to pay to avoid the 'totalizing' effects of social theory.

McHale[11] explains that every theorist and commentator 'constructs' postmodernism in different ways and towards different ends: he also notes that all accounts are 'finally fictitious' – a truly non-referential exercise! McHale also states that postmodernism displays an ontological 'dominant' in opposition and reaction to the 'epistemological' dominant of modernism. This latter distinction is not a disinteresting way to differentiate between phenomena, but it is based upon the binaries that post-structuralism was supposed to have rendered defunct. The binaries also loom large in Harvey's[12] definitions, with modernism addressing *paradigm*, *hypotaxis* and *genital/phallic* formations as opposed to the postmodern preoccupations with *syntagm*, *parataxis* and the *polymorphous/androgenous*. This all contrives to place the postmodern back within the ambit of conventional reason and closed systems of meaning.

However, this continuity will not do. Both Baudrillard and Lyotard, in their different ways, expunge the possible influence of antecedent theorizing by positing an unprecedented fracture between past and present. This assumes a leap into the postmodern which is an extrapolation from a huge conceit, one that Kellner[13] points to, ironically, as a theory of an 'epistemological break' resting itself upon a 'meta-narrative' of the nature of recent history. Baudrillard has prepared us for this failure of continuity through the edict announcing 'the end of society' (this is certainly a development of the Nietzschean valediction for the deity and the Foucauldian reduction of sociology to the role of 'power-knowledge'). The social bond in postmodernity has, it would seem, dispersed into a proliferation of signs and the reality of our being together is fabricated through a series of infinitely reproducible similarities: the simulations of simulacra (surely the hyperbole of Benjamin's shrinking *aura* contained within a vision of the 'eternal recurrence'). History is no longer ordained through human desire and purpose but through an apparently semi-autonomous cybernetic technology. Different but uniform models or codes (transposed from the 'texts' of post-structuralism) come to structure life through social organization. Modernity exploded through 'growth' and 'production' into differences: postmodernity espouses a vertiginous de-differentiation through the implosion into simulations. The consumptive but non-generative 'black hole' becomes a central, and suitably science-fictional, metaphor. Lyotard's postmodernism is a rather more cognitive condition than that of Baudrillard, who though abandoning the ideology of sociology is still inhabiting the same terrain. Lyotard offers us primarily a commentary on knowledge and not a description of social structures, although in many instances it depends implicitly on a Baudrillardian formulation of such structures. He appears concerned to develop an epistemology appropriate to the newly emergent conditions of knowledge, but this is too grand a claim on his behalf. Such theorizing would place him in continuity with the Marxist project of developing historically appropriate categories of understanding. Lyotard reveals himself as resistant to epistemology; he rejects its 'meta-narratives', its backward looking values, its totalizing thought such as that humanistic vision of an altruistic moral commitment inherent in the sociological tradition. In opposition, or substitution, Lyotard recommends the play of 'language games at a local level' – this is the key to rendering the 'now' intelligible. At one point he cites as desirable the replacement of the 'expert's homology' with the 'inventor's parology': could this be an attempt to justify the democratization of all knowledge claims or perhaps a contemporary invocation of the principle of 'falsification'? It is, of course, neither. It is Cartesian radical doubt gone schizoid, and this resonates with the sad, minimalist devastation at the heart of Kroker and Cook's[14] apparition of hyperreal darkness within postmodernism. The message seems to be that in the face of generations of oppressive and exploitative reason and ordered thought, the 'post-' demands faulty logic, mistakes and accident as its methodological imperatives.

This last set of invocations is, sadly, reactive upon the status quo, like the noise of adolescence. Perhaps, as Hutcheon tells us, 'Postmoderism paradoxically manages to legitimize culture (high and low) even as it subverts it'.[15]

Whatever attitude one strikes in relation to the postmodern it cannot be ignored; it is now a cultural phenomenon itself. It has permeated the academy and the media and therefore requires attention. It may be trivialized as mere artefact, 'the decor of a room' or the mini skirt in combination with the army boot, or it can be treated seriously as an endeavour to theorize the 'new' – in progress.

> The difficulties of knowing the contemporary are well known. Knowledge, it is often claimed, can only be gained and enjoyed about what is in some sense over and done with. The claim to know the contemporary is therefore often seen as a kind of conceptual violence, a fixing of the fluid and formless energies of the urgently (but tenuously) present *now* into a knowable and speakable form, by fundamental and irrevocable acts of critical choosing. This formulation rests upon a sense of the inherent division between experience and knowledge, a belief that, when we experience life, we can only partially understand it, and when we try to understand life we are no longer experiencing it. According to this model, knowledge is always doomed to arrive too late on the scene of experience.[16]

However flawed, incomplete or, in places, absurd, this is postmodernism's place, to challenge such disjunction. It is not a body of thought, it is not a method, but it may be an attitude towards culture. Whatever, it is not reducible to axioms, so I shall therefore foolishly attempt its capture around a series of 'family resemblances'.

Postmodernism always begins with the problems set by the 'languaged' character of its culture. It cannot escape, and seeks not to escape, the problems of reference and re-presentation.

Postmodernism witnesses the transformation of the dominant form of knowledge in western society. Science and its ideology – *scientism* – have moved from a belief in the ordered character of externality to a metaphoric relation with the cosmos. As we applaud the shrinkage of 'mind-less' empiricism and 'value-less' positivism, postmodernism addresses the advent of 'techno-science' with its rapidity, calculation, subtlety and intrusiveness. Its ability to imitate and distance the self from whatever reality might have been are exponential.

Baudrillard.

Postmodernism attends to the necessary allegiance of 'techno-science' with national and transnational consumer capitalism. The practical, realist, materiality of everyday life is reduced, through representation, and thus aestheticized.

Postmodernism abandons faith in the 'grand/master/meta-narratives' of traditional epistemologies.

Postmodernism celebrates the previously unspoken (or only whispered) multiplicity of differences of today in sexuality, gender, ethnicity, and art and writing . . . .

Perhaps the 'new European ideal', if not just a resolution of conflict and a policing of difference, would have to be the embodiment of a postmodern culture – timeless, universal, de-contexted, de-traditionalized, spontaneous and impartial symbolism. We will have travelled a long way from a culture which

> . . . includes all the characteristic activities and interests of a people . . . (thus for the English) . . . Derby Day, Henley Regatta, Cowes, the twelfth of August, the cup final, the dog races, the pin table, the dart board, Wensleydale cheese, boiled cabbage cut into sections, beetroot in vinegar, nineteenth-century Gothic churches and the music of Elgar.[17]

NOTES

[1] See Z. Bauman, *Intimations of Postmodernity*, London: Routledge (1992); A. Callinicos, *Against Postmodernism*, Cambridge: Polity (1989); C. Jenks (ed.), *Cultural Reproduction*, London: Routledge (1993).

[2] D. Hebdige, 'A report on the Western Front: postmodernism and the "politics" of style', in C. Jenks, op. cit.

[3] F. Nietzsche, *Thus Spake Zarathustra*, in W. Kaufmann (ed.), *The Portable Nietzsche*, New York: Viking Press (1966), pp. 124–5.

[4] T. Eagleton, *Literary Theory: An Introduction*, Oxford: Blackwell (1983), p. 128.

[5] A. Callinicos, *Is there a Future for Marxism?*, London: Macmillan (1982), p. 46.

[6] D. Hebdige, *Hiding in the Light*, London: Routledge (1988), p. 200.

[7] M. Foucault, 'On Governmentality', *Ideology and Consciousness* 6, 1979, p. 20.

[8] Z. Bauman, 'Is there a postmodern sociology?', *Theory, Culture & Society* Vol. 5 (2–3), 1988, pp. 217.

[9] J.-F. Lyotard, *The Postmodern Condition*, Manchester: Manchester University Press (1984), p. 23.

[10] P. Feyerabend, *Against Method*, London: Verso (1978).

[11] D. McHale, *Postmodernist Fiction*, London: Methuen (1987).

[12] D. Harvey, *The Condition of Postmodernity*, Oxford: Blackwell (1989).

[13] D. Kellner, 'Postmodernism as a social theory: some challenges and problems', *Theory, Culture & Society* Vol. 5, 1988, pp. 239–69.

[14] A. Kroker and D. Cook, *The Postmodern Scene: Excremental Culture and Hyper-aesthetics*, New York: New World Perspectives (1986).

[15] L. Hutcheon, *The Politics of Postmodernism*, London: Routledge (1989), p. 15.

[16] S. Connor, *Postmodernist Culture*, Oxford: Basil Blackwell (1989), p. 3.

[17] T. S. Eliot, *Notes Towards a Definition of Culture*, New York: Harcourt (1948).

8

Cultural studies: what is it?

This book has not been about 'cultural studies' but about the study of culture. The two are not incompatible, but the latter, which subsumes the former, derives from a variety of philosophical antecedents and traditions of social theorizing upon which I have attempted to place some sense of order throughout this short monograph. 'Cultural studies', though drawing variously, and either explicitly or implicitly, from these traditions, is a relative newcomer and claims a difference for itself. I shall attempt here a brief sketch of this difference, or rather identity, and its background, which will not necessarily provide a justification for its particularity although, as in the case of postmodernism, I have confirmed its status by singling it out for special treatment.

Over no more than the last thirty years, initially in Britain and then spreading to North America and Australia, a new realm of research and publication activities has entered the academy under the guise of 'cultural studies'. Within that period it has gained a legitimacy and a popularity, both inside and outside the academy, which is indicative of its appeal to important contemporary social currents. Research centres have been established and have flourished, academic appointments have been made specifically 'in' that field (and one notes this in relation to, say, the significance of Durkheim gaining the first European chair in sociology), graduate and, more recently, undergraduate degree programmes set up, numerous journals launched and heavily subscribed, and publishers have designated lists and promoted editors wholly in terms of 'cultural studies'.

So what is it? If, like Topsy, it just grew, both during the Wilsonian boom in university provision and the support of critical thinking but also through the Thatcher/Joseph period when the social sciences more generally were under threat, then it must surely have strong and influential parentage or the political complexion of a chameleon. Neither of these assessments is strictly true. Over the issue of lineage, Stuart Hall[1] has produced the clearest orthodoxy of a family tree which other, more recent, biographies have assumed as fact and reproduced (and which I shall rehearse in a moment), yet the rush of biographies[2] itself, all prior to even a fiftieth birthday, and a constant 'origins' introspection on the part of even its leading practitioners[3] reveal an orphan child desperately insecure and in search of a parent figure. And over the issue of political complexion one might suggest that the hue was predominantly pink – if not recognizably Marxist then certainly socialist, or at least social-democratic – with a commitment to unfashionable values like conflict and radicalism, reform and democratization. Yet neither of my two previous assessments is strictly false either.

Hall's hagiography for 'cultural studies' points, rightly, to beginnings not so much in continuities as in fractures:

> In serious, critical intellectual work, there are no 'absolute beginnings' and few unbroken continuities. . . . What we find, instead, is an untidy but characteristic unevenness of development. What is important are the significant *breaks* – where old lines of thought are disrupted, older constellations displaced, and elements, old and new, are regrouped around a different set of premises and themes. . . . Cultural Studies, as a distinctive problematic, emerges from one such moment, in the mid-1950's.[4]

It elects a solid triumvirate of men-and-their-texts as formative and epoch-making. The three are Richard Hoggart and his *Uses of Literacy*, Raymond Williams with *Culture and Society* and

E. P. Thompson with *The Making of the English Working Class*. Now this is an impressive group and notable also for its location within the humanities and literary studies, rather than the social sciences. Perhaps part of their acceptability was the capacity to popularize social scientific issues from within 'respectable' disciplines; all three, to varying degrees, were at home within the lecture theatre, the Arts Council, *Late Night LineUp*, the political rally and university administration. All three managed to theorize the social and political grounds of culture without the militant taint of the social sciences, at that time identified with long hair, leather jackets and student occupations. Hoggart, for example, in his Preface, lays out a sociological problematic with a literary 'distancing':

> I am inclined to think that books on popular culture often lose some of their force by not making sufficiently clear who is meant by 'the people', by inadequately relating their examinations of particular aspects of 'the people's' life to the wider life they live, and to attitudes they bring to their entertainments. I have therefore tried to give such a setting, and so far as I could, to describe characteristic working-class relationships and attitudes. Where it is presenting background, this book is based to a large extent on personal experience, and does not purport to have the scientifically-tested character of a sociological survey. There is an obvious danger of generalization from limited experience. I have therefore included, chiefly in notes, some of the findings of sociologists where they seemed necessary, either as support or as qualification of the text. I have also one or two instances in which others, with experiences similar to mine, think differently.[5]

Nevertheless, Hoggart, Williams and Thompson are collected, by Hall, as the '*caesura*' out of which 'cultural studies' sprang because all three treated working-class culture (with a disregard for the 'culture debate' over high/low or mass) as active, coherent, intelligible, located within history, and – even though all three work with versions of materialism – not solely reducible to a developing set of economic conditions. This important sense of 'agency' in culture is well established by Thompson when he tells us that the growth of the working class

. . . is revealed, first, in the growth of class consciousness: the consciousness of an identity of interests as between all these diverse groups of working people and as against the interests of other classes. And, second, in the growth of corresponding forms of political and industrial organization. By 1832 there were strongly-based and self-conscious working-class institutions – trade unions, friendly societies, educational and religious movements, political organisations, periodicals – working-class intellectual traditions, working-class community-pattern, and a working-class structure of feeling.[6]

They did not arise as a necessary by-product of the factory system.

It is, of course, possible to overemphasize the communality of vision between these three figures. Hoggart's recollections of Hunslett are deeply impressionistic and carry, within their care and anger, a romanticism bordering on sentimentality. The upshot of this is a model of culture which, although vibrant and valuable in its own right, is nevertheless passive, receptive and tending towards complacency. Williams has a much more voluntaristic view of culture and sees it as a dynamic. But despite his illumination of working-class culture as real and not merely the overshadowed residue in a high-culture dominated society, his Leavis-like view of culture as a totality incorporates the former and enables it to contribute, thus deradicalizing its potential. Thompson, Marxist from the outset, forbids the notion of a common culture and predicates his account on autonomy, challenge, conflict and, above all, class struggle.

Hall, beyond introducing Hoggart, Williams and Thompson as forebears of 'cultural studies', further divides its contemporary practice between 'two paradigms' – the *culturalist* and the *structuralist*, the difference being that in culturalism 'the stress is placed on the *making* of culture rather than on its determined conditions' and in structuralism 'the stress is placed on the specific nature of those supposedly irreducible formal properties which characterize the structure of different types of signifying practice and distinguish them one from another'.[7]

The triumvirate are all culturalists and the structuralists, though an imprecise category, are broadly followers of de Saussure, like Lévi-Strauss, Foucault and Barthes all discussed earlier. Hall's two paradigms live on, though less contentiously than before, with the British historicists resisting the generalizing and decontextualizing theoreticity of the structuralists with their all too comprehensive and deterministic conception of ideology. However, the development of a neo-Gramscian perspective through the work of the Birmingham Centre for Contemporary Cultural Studies, under the directorship of Hall himself, meant that a softer mediation between agency and all-encompassing structure was provided through the concept of *hegemony*. 'Cultural studies' was saved from an early, and wasteful, internecine conflict. It was the establishment of the Birmingham Centre for Contemporary Cultural Studies (CCCS), initially under Richard Hoggart and then most notably under Stuart Hall for over a decade, that probably did more than any other intellectual or institutional initiative in this country to provide a solid and recognizable foundation for what is now known as 'cultural studies'. The CCCS generated a shared problematic (the Gramscian sense of ideology), a set of, albeit loose, methods and strategies for research (such as ethnography), a particular range or perhaps strata of substantive topics (like 'subcultures') and a group of young, ambitious and multi-disciplinary theorists sprouting out of an imaginative postgraduate programme into film, media, cultural and communication studies departments and providing a momentum of enthusiasm, research and publication that has not waned up to the present. In this way the CCCS itself has constituted the 'third paradigm' of 'cultural studies', and its network.

Referring back to Hall's sense of 'old lines of thought', we might suggest three other contributions to, or starting points for, modern 'cultural studies' which though not unexplored remain unacknowledged in their lineage. The first is a near contemporary of the triumvirate, namely, George Orwell. His observations on popular fiction in relation to a sense of the 'dominant ideology', his analyses of the absence of a working-class presence in nineteenth-century fiction (other than through the representation of a 'mob'), his falsely prophetic *1984* views on mass culture/mass audience through the ever increasing power and penetration of the mass media, and his Hoggart-like romanticism in reconstructing working-class community and home life would all seem to qualify him for, at least, a passing reference on the road to 'cultural studies':

In a working-class home . . . you breathe a warm, decent, deeply human atmosphere which is not so easy

> to find elsewhere. I should say that a manual worker, if
> he is in steady work and drawing good wages . . . has a
> better chance of being happy than an 'educated' man.[8]

The second source derives from the late nineteenth and early twentieth century and has a substantive rather than a theoretic core. This is the Victorian 'centre' for contemporary cultural studies, the 'centre' being the East End of London and its contributions being Henry Mayhew's *London Labour and the London Poor*, Jack London's *People of the Abyss*, Charles Booth's *Life and Labour of People in London*, Walter Besant's *East London*, James Greenwood's *Low Life Deeps*, the novels of Charles Dickens and Arthur Morrison, and the writings of Henry James, Mearns, Sims, Engels and many, many more. These urban spectators picked up on and gave voice to the outcast and inarticulate culture of a working class delineated and ghettoized morally, politically, economically, and even geographically and architecturally. Their work is informed by no clear theory of ideology but by a 'bitter cry' on behalf of 'the whole way of life of a people' informed by observation, demography and epidemiology. Their practices have been most cynically described in terms that modern 'cultural studies' would equally well need to refute:

> . . . 'being at home in the city' was represented as a
> privileged gaze, betokening possession and distance, that
> structured 'a range of disparate texts and heterogeneous
> practices which emerge in the nineteenth century city –
> tourism, exploration/discovery, social investigation, social
> policy'.
>
> A powerful streak of voyeurism marked all of these
> activities; the 'zeal for reform' was often accompanied
> 'by a prolonged, fascinated gaze' from the bourgeoisie.[9]

The *flâneur*, both ancient and modern.

The final source of neglected antecedents derives from sociology in the USA and has two tributaries. The first leads from the isolated East Coast study published in 1943 by William Foote Whyte and called *Street Corner Society*. This is now hailed as a classic sociological exercise in the methodology borrowed from anthropology, known as 'participant observation'. Whyte lived for a number of years with an Italian-American gang, as a quasi-member, initially engaging in their nefarious activities and at all times eliciting their cooperation and support in his study of their shared lives.

The second comes from the neo-Chicago School, that following in the wake of G. H. Mead, Park and Burgess, came under the leadership of Everett C. Hughes and involved such figures as Becker, Roth, Geer, Strauss, Davis and Goffman. All of these middle-class students were 'encouraged' to carry out their postgraduate research in the form of participant observation, through living in and acting out social roles that would otherwise be wholly foreign to them. They have provided us with a series of sensitive and subjective accounts of the symbolic interaction involved in being a cab-driver, a trainee nurse, a hairdresser, a TB patient, a jazz musician and even a drug user. Their sense of the politic behind their 'cultural' studies is captured in their phrase 'the sociology of the underdog'.

So, cultural studies: what is it? I shall conclude with a list of attributes deriving from Agger's formulation.[10]

1   Cultural studies operates with an expanded concept of culture. It rejects the assumptions behind the 'culture debate' and thus rejects the high/low culture binary or, indeed, any attempt to re-establish the grounds for any cultural stratification. It adheres more closely to the anthropological view of culture as being 'the whole way of life of a people', though it does not subscribe to the view of culture as a totality.

2   Following from the above, cultural studies legitimates, justifies, celebrates and politicizes all aspects of popular culture. It regards popular culture as valuable in its own right and not a 'shadow phenomenon' or simply a vehicle for ideological mystification.

3   The proponents of cultural studies, as representative of their age, recognize the socialization of their own identities through the processes of mass media and communication that they seek to understand.

4   Culture is not viewed in stasis, as fixed or as a closed system. Cultural studies regards culture as emergent, as dynamic and as continual renewal. Culture is not a series of artefacts or frozen symbols but rather a process.

5   Cultural studies is predicated upon conflict rather than order. It investigates, and anticipates, conflict both at the level of face-to-face interaction but also, and more significantly, at the level of meaning. Culture cannot be viewed as a unifying

principle, a source of shared understanding or a mechanism for legitimating the social bond.

6 Cultural studies is 'democratically' imperialistic. As all aspects of social life are now 'cultured' then no part of social life is excluded from its interests – opera, fashion, gangland violence, pub talk, shopping, horror films and so on . . . they are no longer colonized, canonized or zoned around a central meaning system.

7 Cultural representations are viewed by cultural studies at all levels – inception, mediation and reception, or production, distribution and consumption.

8 Cultural studies is interdisciplinary, it acknowledges no disciplinary origin, it encourages work on the interface of disciplinary concerns and it acknowledges a shifting and sprightly muse.

9 Cultural studies rejects absolute values – it does what it wants (and sometimes, it shows!).

NOTES

[1] S. Hall, 'Cultural studies: two paradigms', in T. Bennett, G. Martin, C. Mercer and J. Woollacott, *Culture, Ideology and Social Process*, London: Open University/Batsford (1981).

[2] G. Turner, *British Cultural Studies*, London: Unwin Hyman (1990); B. Agger, *Cultural Studies as Critical Theory*, London: Falmer (1992).

[3] R. Johnson, 'What is cultural studies anyway?' CCCs stencilled paper No. 74 (1983).

[4] S. Hall, op. cit., p. 19

[5] R. Hoggart, *The Uses of Literacy*, Harmondsworth: Penguin (1958), p. 9.

[6] E. P. Thompson, *The Making of the English Working Class*, Harmondsworth: Penguin (1968).

[7] T. Bennett *et al.*, op. cit., pp. 10–11.

[8] G. Orwell, *The Road to Wigan Pier*, London: Gollancz (1937).

[9] G. Pollock, quoted in J. Walkowitz, *City of Dreadful Delights*, London: Virago (1992), p. 16.

[10] B. Agger, op. cit.

9

Cultural deprivation: a case study in conceptual confusion

The salient point contained in this case study is an elaboration of the predominant divergence in the conceptualization of culture that has run throughout this text, namely the split between the notions of culture as being (a) descriptive of the whole pattern of representations of a recognizable and coherent group of people, and (b) referential of the specialized and self-selected excellence of the creative potential of a recognizable and coherent group of people. Here I wish to show a real, but exaggerated, instance of the eliding and thus confusing of the difference between these two conceptualizations, for reasons that are complexes of the moral, the political, and also of incoherent thinking; all of which instance the necessity of clarity in realizing our shared problematic – 'culture'.

This case study makes reference to the once fashionable and politically correct concerns, in educational policy, with the issue of 'cultural deprivation'. This is a topic that has figured largely in the thinking of the sociology of education since the 1950s.

To attain an understanding of the 'normative' basis of much of the traditional approach to the sociology of education, during its relatively brief career, it is important to attend to the wider issue of making explicit the assumptions and value judgements that are inherent in social theory more generally. Social theories, particularly if they are to be used to provide the rationale for policy action, are conventionally treated as 'information'. That is to say that, for the purposes of practical application, such theories are treated as uncontestable, empirical generalizations which are neutral in respect of value. In this way, it is assumed, they become amenable for a bias-free application onto a constant, and receptive, social world. In this way, whatever is contained within the theory is taken as reflecting the real state of affairs in the world, so long as it is coherent with the '*Weltanschauung*' of the policy administrators.

Now, my contention, and that held by much contemporary sociological analysis, is that such theorizing is not, and cannot be, free from the judgements of value built into the constitution of what are regarded as 'facts'. All social theories define and explain human conduct from socially situated value positions – in this sense they are 'normative' (that is, their 'truth' coheres with what is a dominant, taken-for-granted view of the world). We might suggest then, that all social theories are fashioned by the professional view and the political ideologies of their theorists – which, in turn, may be sustained and appreciated in terms of particular forms of knowledge and interests that are inherent within the status quo. This will clearly be the case if the theory remains uncritical of the status quo.

If we return this issue to the context of education, we can provide an analysis of the normative assumptions inherent in certain forms of theorizing by looking at one formulation of the social problem known as 'educational failure', that is, the seeming failure of individuals to realize their true potential through the formal agencies of socialization, like schools. As social theorists we must not look at the conventional sense of this issue but rather at its sociological character – so our explanations are in terms of structures of facilitation or inhibition rather than in terms of the inadequacies or pathologies of particular learners. Now, concretely, this analysis will involve the dissembling of the form of educational policy that came to be known as 'compensatory education'; and 'compensatory education' rests on a diffuse and ill-considered theory of 'cultural deprivation'.

A dominant theme of educational reform in this country, up until the 1980s, had been the extension of educational opportunity to wider, and yet wider, sections of the community, with the aim of counteracting the dominant structural forms of stratification in society, such as social class, race, gender, disability and even age. However, even a modest realization of the conditions of formal equality in educational practice has done little to eliminate educational privilege. Despite changes in selection, teaching and the organization of knowledge, many children, because of aspects of their life experience, appear unable, or unwilling, to take advantage of the opportunities now open to them. Thus attention turned not simply to the removal of formal barriers but further to a provision of special privileges for those perceived as 'handicapped' in terms of achievement. In many ways this 'special provision' for the needy was not new; the early Victorian philanthropists clearly recognized that hunger and ill-health impede learning, and indeed any motivation to achieve, and following this recognition the English education system came to provide a physical baseline for all of its pupils through free school milk (later withdrawn by Mrs Thatcher, then Minister for Education), school meals and school health services. However, in more recent years the problems of educational failure were seen to go beyond merely physical needs, and the programmes of remedial care shifted from special provision, through active compensation, to the ideologically acute positive discrimination. Our topic here is the era of active compensation.

THE CONCEPT OF CULTURAL DEPRIVATION

In substantive terms, the concept of 'cultural deprivation' sought to address the problem, as conceived by some groups of teachers and educational administrators, of the educational malfunctioning of certain targeted groups of children, defined by their membership of particular social groupings, most specifically social class and ethnic origin. Although, in this country, the Plowden Report of 1967 noted the appalling conditions and lack of facilities in many of our local primary schools and recommended 'positive discrimination' of resources through the network of 'educational priority areas', this was already a late stage in the development of the troubled concept.

The concept of *cultural deprivation* arose in the USA during the 1950s. Though largely pragmatic in origin it emerged as a high-profile strategy within the Federal Government's 'war on poverty' and combined with other elements in the Kennedys' campaign to claim the moral high ground and mobilize the growing liberalism of the time as part of its power base. This 'war on poverty' came about through a manifestly economic concern with the depressed material circumstances of certain politically sensitive groups in America, such as the poor whites, the North American Indians, and particularly the masses of lower-class Black people who no longer languished in the cotton fields and the Mississippi delta but who threatened to burst out of their cramped containment within the inner-city ghettos. The social circumstances of all of these groups were seen, quite accurately, to correlate systematically with unemployment, crime, delinquency and educational failure. This burden of negative symbolism associated with such group membership was becoming an obvious stain on the American culture of the 'free' and the 'brave'. All of these pathological manifestations were conceived of as being, at least, counter-productive or, at most, positively threatening features in relation to the stability and successful maintenance of the social system (as Parsons would have recognized it). Thus, the 'sub-standard' citizenship of these groups of people became the site of corrective practices and the topic of remedial attention.

COMPENSATORY EDUCATION

The major theme of the 'compensatory education' movement was seen as the alleviation of low educational performance; and whatever the origins of the movement this theme tied in well with the dominant ideology in the USA, with 'achievement', in whatever realm, always being realized as the American dream. As with all normatively oriented systems of thought, new categories of pathology or deviant were created in its wake. In this instance the categories were educational categories, and thus a new vocabulary of diagnosis entered into the discourse of educators. We now had 'culturally deprived' children, 'linguistically deprived' children and 'socially disadvantaged' children. Programmes of compensatory education were established with the sole, explicit, aim of altering the status of 'these kinds of children'. These programmes were well-funded policy measures committed to the transformation of the child's identity from one level of potential to another; or some might suggest, from one level of being to another. Largely, such programmes were directed by educational psychologists, and the existence, or indeed the definitional characteristics of 'cultural deprivation' was never for one moment held in question. If we look at the opening paragraph of Riessman's influential work *The Culturally Deprived Child* he states;

> In 1950, approximately one child out of every ten in the fourteen largest cities of the United States was 'culturally deprived'. By 1960, this figure had risen to one in three. This ever increasing trend is due to their rapid migration to urban centres. By 1970, it is estimated there may be one deprived child for every two enrolled in schools in these large cities. . . . Clearly one of the most pressing problems facing the urban school today is the 'culturally deprived child'.[1]

And he footnotes on the opening page: 'The terms "culturally deprived", "educationally deprived", "deprived", "underprivileged", "disadvantaged", "lower class", "lower socio-economic group" are used interchangeably throughout this book.'[2]

Such was the reality that the educational world presented itself with. Contemporary disbelief at the general acceptance of such thinking during the 1950s and 1960s is provided with some insight by Friedman[3] who goes some way towards explaining the politically contexted plausibility of such insipience. Friedman explains that when 'cultural deprivation' theory was linked with policy action it interpellated the interests of diverse and contradictory groups within the American polity. It had an appeal to various ideological persuasions; liberals saw it as positive and constructive reform, a kind of morally grounded remedial largesse that would advance the progress of high profile minority groups; conservatives, on the other hand, saw it as an exercise in governance and containment; it would be instrumental in 'keeping the slum kids straight' and 'cooling out the social dynamite in the ghetto'.

The causal reasoning of the 'cultural deprivation' theorists may be formulated as follows: a child's educability (that is, the child's propensity to achieve in an education system that is regarded as constant and, in itself, unproblematic) is to be accounted for largely in terms of early socialization and factors antecedent to his or her in-school experience. The more negative, and perhaps more accurate, formulation of their position is: a poor white/Afro-American/native-American child's relative failure at school is traceable to his or her home background and upbringing. By not taking into account the school as an agency in the creation of success and failure, and as an agency in the transmission of 'culture', most programmes and research in this area can be seen to have provided ideological support for a particular white, middle-class, elitist view of what constitutes 'culture' which is embodied in an implicit, and assumed, consensus view of the social order. This, in turn, provides the basis for a classification of children and their families along an axis from normality to social pathology, which is reflected symbolically through cultural stratification.

As Bernstein put it, in a paper properly dissociating his own work from the invidious network of muddled thinking:

> The concept 'compensatory education' serves to direct attention away from the internal organization of the educational context of the school, and focus our attention upon the families and children. The concept 'compensatory education' implies that something is lacking in the family, and so in the child. As a result the children are unable to benefit from schools. It follows then that the school has to 'compensate' for the something which is missing in the family, and the children are looked at as deficit systems. If only the parents were interested in the goodies we offer, if only they were like middle-class parents, then we could do our job. Once the problem is seen even implicitly this way, then it becomes appropriate to coin the terms 'cultural deprivation', 'linguistic deprivation', etc. And then these labels do their own sad work.
>
> If children are labelled 'culturally deprived', then it follows that the parents are inadequate, the spontaneous realizations of their culture, its images and symbolic representations are of reduced value and significance.[4]

Given all of the analytic complexity attaching to the use of the concept of 'culture' that has been demonstrated in our work so far within this text, we can readily observe the dangers that follow from the ill-considered view of culture that was at work within this context. At least there was the indelicacy of conceptual confusion and at worst there was the political mal-distribution of resources and the systematic symbolic violence that was exercised (for all the best reasons) on the identities of the children involved, and on their family relations.

MAINSTREAM CULTURE

By stressing the child as a problem with reference to a singular, and yet opaque, notion of culture, the 'cultural deprivation' theorists' position assumes that to be successful in the education system is, at least, to bring to the school situation, certain values, ideas and beliefs – what we might call cultural sentiments – which are in tune with the 'mainstream culture' of that society. Now this new concept, the 'mainstream culture', is the grandest confusion of all. It refers, in as much as it has a referent, to the way of life of a people, but only the normative way of life of a people, and also to the best elements of that way of life of a people. It is really a quiet description of the dominant ideology. Practically it was assumed that the 'mainstream culture' was typically manifested in the forms of knowledge, teaching styles and established role behaviours in the school as an institution embodying that culture; in this way it is a circular and self-confirming concept. Likewise, 'culturally deprived' children were those who were unable to bring these basic requisites to the school situation; they were ironically and inevitably 'deprived' of the culture within which success can be realized.

Let us now continue through the logic of the 'cultural deprivation' theorists, and pay special attention to the character of the metaphors employed in their discourse. Their methodology demanded that in order to 'aid' the deprived, to provide 'enrichment' in their pre-school life, to 'compensate' for their upbringing, and to provide an 'antidote' to their minority group, and thus, anti-educational culture, such children needed to be provided with a pre-school education that would counteract what their families had done for them. So the 'deprivationists' were committed to counterbalancing the negative influences of the child's home environment. Such practice, it was supposed, would bring 'culturally deprived' children up to par as potential educatees by providing them with a crash course in 'mainstream culture'.

To take an example of an actual, and influential, policy programme, *Project Head Start* started in the USA in July 1965. This project was concerned with 'early childhood intervention', which consisted of pre-school, 'deprived' children (who were initially selected from social workers' lists in ghetto districts) being admitted to 'Child Development Centres' for an eight-week session in the summer prior to the commencement of their initial schooling. No uniform curriculum was developed in such centres, but Osborn, writing in 1966, stated that the activities in most centres were comprised of artwork, stories, creative play, science projects and visits to various cultural sources and community facilities: 'Many situations which the middle-class children take for granted Head Start children experience for the first time. Many of these youngsters had never had a book read to them.'[5]

Class, here, is clearly being realized as the critical basis for the acquisition or non-acquisition of culture and this is an important slippage and reformulation within the original theory. A central feature of the concept 'cultural deprivation' was that, in effect, it took life as a psychologistic construct which was aimed at the explanation of some modes of child development and personality maturation, but explicitly at the level of the individual. As the concept grew and flourished its political impact would have been diminished if it had continued to explain through a fragmented atomism and it therefore assumed the status of a more general, more sociological concept, which elevated its subject to the realm of a social problem worthy of policy measures and resource implications.

In practice, the initial eight-week sessions of cultural improvement were demonstrably ineffective, but although the period of pre-school training was progressively lengthened beyond the original two-month period Project Head Start was generally judged not to have achieved any significant results. How, indeed, could it? The absurd logic of such 'intervention' would lead to snatching the child away from the mother at birth in order to dispense with the family's failure to correctly transmit culture, or to transmit culture at all. Freidman[6] quotes from what he regards as a fairly typical portrait of the 'culturally deprived child' from the literature of the period:

> . . . he is essentially the child who has been isolated from those rich experiences that should be his. This isolation may be brought about by poverty, by meagreness of intellectual resources in his home and surroundings, by the incapacity, illiteracy or indifference of his elders or the entire community. He may have come to school without ever having had his mother sing him the traditional lullabies, and with no knowledge of nursery rhymes, fairy stories, or the folk-lore of his country. He may have taken few trips – perhaps the only one the cramped,

uncomfortable trip from the lonely shack on the tenant farm to the teaming, filthy slum dwelling – he probably knows nothing of poetry, painting, music or even indoor plumbing.[7]

It requires little expert knowledge to recognize the classist and racist attitudes paraded quite explicitly here in the spurious attempt to distinguish good and bad parenting in relation to the transmission of 'culture'.

Freidman also quotes from a psychologist writing under the title 'The psychological basis for using pre-school enrichment as an antidote to cultural deprivation':

. . . cultural deprivation may be seen as a failure to provide an opportunity for infants and young children to have the experiences required for adequate development of those semi-autonomous central processes demanded for acquiring skill in the use of linguistic and mathematical symbols and for the analysis of causal relationships. The difference between the culturally deprived child and the culturally privileged is, for children, analogous to the difference between cage-reared and pet-reared rats and dogs.[8]

Apart from the offensive, reverse anthropomorphism, this quote is also notable for its juxtapositioning of 'privileged' with 'deprived', and the invocation of the notion of 'antidote' to some assumed, albeit metaphoric, sense of poisoning. Given the tone of some of these extracts it is not hard to imagine some of the critiques that arose from both 'cultural deprivation' programmes and the thinking behind them. The movement itself was viewed by many as an obstacle to civil rights and a device to impose white, middle-class values on the population as a whole. At the conceptual level there is a noticeable, and even calculated, vagueness, and a high degree of theoretical inadequacy. The major point in relation to our set of concerns in elucidating the idea of culture is a sustained disregard of the distinction between 'cultural difference' and 'cultural deficit'; or to put that another way, a conflation of the distinction between a sociological concept of culture as signifying the way of life of a people, and the aesthetic and hierarchical concept which signifies the best that a civilization has, over time, achieved. Thus, even if we were to accept some sense of 'deprivation', as being a lack of that which is important and necessary, it is causally simplistic to deduce a universal societal reaction or manifestation, like, for example, educational failure. Such thinking glosses over the more complex structural issues of segregation and the ideology of white supremacy, the practical issues of differential material provision, and the political issues involved in educational practice itself. Thus what becomes apparent from the notion of 'enrichment' and the resonances of the interventionists' metaphors generally is a confusion in their use of the concept of culture. While manifestly operating with an idea of culture in a sociological/anthropological sense, they are implicitly drawing upon a specialized version of culture, as 'high culture', which accounts for their references to poetry, music, painting, stories and so on; this latter is culture as heritage.

The idea of culture implies a notion of accumulated, shared symbols, representative of and significant within a particular society. A culture is a contexted semiotic system. As such the reality which the concept summons up is in no sense a fixed material entity. It would seem singularly unamenable to quantification, therefore to endow individuals with more or less access to or accumulation of culture (as in privileged versus deprived) is somewhat absurd. Everybody has culture, and is with culture, in that they are social beings; it is an instance of their member-shipping, culture being a collective symbol of social existence. Thus, we should ask, can children be culturally deprived, or just different (i.e. not necessarily in deficit)? To produce this difference as a ranking between people is to produce a stratification on grounds that are unexplicated within the theorizing of the interventionists. In one sense they accomplish this manoeuvre by the introduction of the idea of a 'mainstream culture'. This stands as the assumed, dominant, consensus culture of a society, which provides the yardstick against which an individual's 'deprivation' may be assessed. As Keddie informs us:

> Commonly the child is conceived of as an object with attributes that can be measured, so that the focus has been on creating, for example, objective measures of ability, rather than on interactional contexts and on teachers' ways of assessing and typifying students and the ways in which teachers and students interpret and give meaning to educational situations.[9]

In many ways this concept 'mainstream culture' resonates with a Parsonian scheme of dominant central value systems; it also presupposes a strong theory of culture and a rigid consensus model of the social, which forbids diversity. The analytic problem remains, whose culture is mainstream? Thus, in terms of what, by whose definition, are other individuals relatively deprived? What, indeed, are the rules of a 'mainstream culture'? This issue is continuously ignored or taken for granted in the contemporary literature. The empirical manifestations of a 'mainstream culture' would seem to be the attributes of the successful: as such, it is a tautology. The confused picture that emerges from the literature would seem to indicate that 'mainstream culture' = Standard English Speech = All American Boy = WASP = middle-class white = what large sections of the population are not, by definition.

Standard English Speech developed as the second, and yet rather more subtle, conceptual measure employed by the interventionists to assess 'cultural deprivation'. It is subtle because it is tangible, ever present, and (as every good English person knows) language and language use is a certain, albeit commonsensical, testimony to the 'real' person. Standard English Speech thus came to be regarded as the linguistic realization of 'mainstream culture'. It was taken to represent that aspect of the central value system which referred to linguistic convention and, therefore, a rule against which 'linguistic deprivation' might be measured.

STANDARD ENGLISH SPEECH

Another series of conceptual conflations occurred around the idea of the 'cultured person' being able to articulate their world view, and express their unique intent. It was as if lexical choices (and accent) maketh man. Important pioneering work in sociolinguistics, such as that of Bernstein, was invoked here as the theoretical foundations of such assumptions. This was a role that Bernstein vociferously repudiated. However, the new reality of Standard English Speech had become established; so, we need to ask, where then do we find SES spoken, and by whom? What are its rules? The work on 'linguistic deprivation', as an aspect of 'cultural deprivation', was largely based on an examination of linguistic rules rather than socio-linguistic rules. That is to say that it was grammar, not speech, that was addressed in the analyses of the interventionists. SES was judged to be assessable in terms of an abstract, and yet highly normative, compliance with grammatical forms and syntactical rules. As a consequence speech, performance, became diminished in importance and meaning as situated action was wholly disregarded. However, as Cicourel[10] has later pointed out, we are only able to make *post hoc* assessments of language competence in terms of language performance (in the form of situated speech). To achieve successful, that is meaningful, talk, or rational speech behaviour, in a social setting is due to social competence, or membership, or the ability to be part of a shared 'culture'.

Another significant critique of the notion of 'linguistic deprivation' is provided by the work of Torrey where she informs us that:

> Although Standard English serves as the medium of instruction in reading and other subjects and is the only dialect accepted as 'correct' in the dominant society, the deviations of many black children from the standard forms cannot be regarded as errors. These so called 'errors' actually conform to discernible grammatical rules, different from those of the standard language, but no less systematic. Furthermore, the patterns of black children's grammar that strike the Standard English-speaking teacher as incomplete, illogical or linguistically retarded actually conform closely to rules of adult language spoken in the Ghetto.[11]

Thus the exclusion enabled through the generation of a regime of judgement in the name of Standard English creates an insensitivity, or even a blindness, towards the regularities and conformities in the speech patterns of minority groups (or cultures). As Torrey further suggests, language carries two functions, the intellectual and the social. The former enables the successful passage of communication, and the latter provides for membership and identification of, conversely, exclusion and stigmatization.

Finally, we may look at Labov's[12] contribution to the debate over 'linguistic', and by implication 'cultural', deprivation. He demonstrates that tests and interviews conducted to determine reading skills and linguistic competence in children are inappropriate, and discriminatory, since they seek to match all different children's socio-linguistic performance against a partial and idealized model of language structure – that is, the grammatical rules of Standard English. Thus when a child responds to the interview situation, as some do, with defensive, withdrawn, monosyllabic behaviour, Labov interprets this as rational, competent behaviour by children who are feeling threatened. When children perceive themselves to be in a situation in which anything they say can literally be written down and used in evidence against them, they artfully employ a number of devices to avoid speaking. Such interviews are then, in reality, demonstrations of children's ability to defend themselves in a hostile environment (an in-school experience perhaps not uncommon for some large groups within the population). Nevertheless, the outcome of such interviews are regarded, within the rhetoric of the deprivationists, as fair measures of the individual child's total verbal capacity; and it is extrapolated from this that lack of verbality explains poor performance in schools. Labov retaliates by setting up more sympathetic and inviting interview situations, in terms of ethnic bias or even sheer relaxation, and produces dramatically altered test results. His point, however, is clear: the interview situation might be regarded, for some groups of children, as a microcosm of their whole educational life – not deprived but intimidated and excluded through difference. Such children may themselves regard their speech form to be systematically stigmatized (or offered antidotes) in school; this does not mean that it is inadequate for communication.

We return to the position of asking, where do we find and how do we recognize Standard English Speech? In terms of whose behaviour and lifestyles do we typify 'mainstream culture', and in what sense is it mainstream such that others may be judged significantly different and thus 'deprived' in relation to it?

'Mainstream culture' appears as a concept but is, in fact, a typed construct, implicity opposed to the culture (as defined) of the individual or group under consideration and perceived as 'minority', 'deviant', 'deprived' or 'sub-cultural'. Its conceptual confusion provides a contrived basis for ethnocentrism as a standpoint in the interventionists' practices. The method of their policy produces differences as morally significant, it enables and reinforces a spurious ranking, which nevertheless has serious implications for the lives of the people so stratified.

People, in their groups, are different and diverse, all according to a multiplicity of sets of criteria, one set of which generates the idea of 'culture', as we have seen throughout this book. As social and cultural theorists we should reflexively examine the social construction of the criteria and not the supposed intrinsic qualities, or pathologies, of the people classified in relation to them. This is an important analytic issue. The cultural deprivationists' confusion arose from their particular perspective, thus what they claimed to know about cultural difference, rather than being independent of their ways of coming to know, may now be seen as being generated by those very processes of coming to know. Different concepts, of culture or whatever; different methods, different forms of theorizing themselves, create different orders of relevance. All worlds, and cultures, are fashioned as such.

NOTES

[1] F. Riessman, *The Culturally Deprived Child*, New York: Harper and Row (1962), p. 1.

[2] Ibid., p. 1.

[3] N. L. Friedman, 'Cultural deprivation: a commentary on the sociology of knowledge', in J. Beck, C. Jenks, N. Keddie and M. F. D. Young, *Worlds Apart – Readings for a Sociology of Education*, London: Collier-Macmillan (1977), pp. 120–33.

[4] B. Bernstein, 'A critique of the concept of compensatory education', in D. Rubenstein and C. Stoneman (eds), *Education for Democracy*, Harmondsworth: Penguin (1970), p. 112.

[5] Osborn, cited in N. L. Friedman, op. cit.

[6] N. L. Friedman, op. cit.

[7] C. K. Brooks, 'Some approaches to teaching English as a second language', in S. W. Webster (ed), *The Disadvantaged Learner*, San Francisco: Chandler (1966), p. 516–17.

[8] J. McVicker-Hunt, 'The psychological basis for using pre-school enrichment as an antidote for cultural deprivation', *Merrill-Palmer Quarterly*, 10 July 1964, p. 236.

[9] N. Keddie (ed.), *Tinker, Tailor . . . the Myth of Cultural Deprivation*, Harmondsworth: Penguin (1977), p. 15.

[10] A. Cicourel, 'The acquisition of social structure: toward a developmental sociology of language and meaning', in J. Douglas (ed.), *Understanding Everyday Life*, London: Routledge & Kegan Paul (1971).

[11] J. Torrey, 'Illiteracy in the Ghetto', in N. Keddie, op. cit.

[12] W. Labov, 'The logic of non-standard English', in N. Keddie, op. cit.

Further reading

Each chapter contains references to the original texts, sources of quotations, and some secondary sources which have been drawn on. All of these are recommended reading. Listed below are important background sources not cited elsewhere.

CHAPTER 1

Archer, M. S. (1988) *Culture and Agency*, Cambridge: Cambridge University Press.

Bauman, Z. (1973) *Culture as Praxis*, London: Routledge & Kegan Paul.

Billington, R., Strawbridge, S., Greensides, L. and Fitzsimons, A. (1991) *Culture and Society*, London: Macmillan.

Ulin, R. (1984) *Understanding Cultures*, Austin: University of Texas Press.

Williams, R. (1987) *Culture and Society: Coleridge to Orwell*, London: Hogarth Press.

CHAPTER 2

Diamond, S. (1980) *Anthropology: Ancestors and Heirs*, The Hague: Mouton.

Langness, L. L. (1974) *The Study of Culture*, Novato, CA: Chandler and Sharp.

CHAPTER 3

Lévi-Strauss, C. (1969a) *Totemism*, Harmondsworth: Penguin.

Lévi-Strauss, C. (1969b) *The Elementary Structure of Kinship*, London: Eyre and Spottiswood.

Outhwaite, W. (1975) *Understanding Social Life*, London: Allen and Unwin.

CHAPTER 4

Evans, M. (1981) *Lucien Goldmann*, Brighton: Harvester.

Frisby, D. (1985) *Fragments of Modernity*, Cambridge: Polity.

Joll, J. (1977) *Gramsci*, Glasgow: Fontana.

Lovell, T. (1980) *Pictures of Reality*, London: British Film Institute.

Williams, R. (1977) *Marxism and Literature*, Oxford: Oxford University Press.

Williams, R. (1979) *Politics and Letters*, London: New Left Books.

Williams, R. (1980) *Problems in Materialism and Culture*, London: Verso.

CHAPTER 5

Bell, M. (1988) *F. R. Leavis*, London: Routledge.

Boyers, R. (1978) *F. R. Leavis*, Columbia: University of Missouri Press.

Eliot, T. S. (1948) *Notes Towards the Definition of Culture*, London: Faber and Faber.

Hayman, R. (1976) *Leavis*, London: Heinemann.

Jay, M. (1973) *The Dialectical Imagination*, Boston: Little, Brown.

CHAPTER 6

Bourdieu, P. (1979) *Distinction*, London: Routledge & Kegan Paul.

CHAPTER 7

Baudrillard, J. (1988) *Selected Writings*, ed. M. Poster, Cambridge: Polity.

Featherstone, M. (1988) *Theory, Culture & Society*, special issue on 'postmodernism', Vol. 5, nos. 2–3.

Foster, H. (1983) *The Anti-Aesthetic: Essays on Postmodern Culture*, Port Townsend, WA: Bay Press.

CHAPTER 8

Easthope, A. (1991) *Literary into Cultural Studies*, London: Routledge.

Wuthnow, R., Hunter, J. D., Bergesen, A. and Kurzweil, E. (1984) *Cultural Analysis*, London: Routledge & Kegan Paul.

CHAPTER 9

All relevant material is cited in the text.

Name index

Subject index